NO FINAL SOLUTION

Other Mainstream titles by the same author:

*Blood on the Thistle: A Casebook of 20th-century Scottish Murder*
*Frightener: The Glasgow Ice-cream Wars*, with Lisa Brownlie

# NO FINAL SOLUTION

# SOLUTION

## Unsolved Crimes of the Twentieth Century

DOUGLAS
SKELTON

MAINSTREAM
PUBLISHING

EDINBURGH AND LONDON

First published in Great Britain in 1994 by
MAINSTREAM PUBLISHING COMPANY
(EDINBURGH) LTD
7 Albany Street
Edinburgh EH1 3UG

ISBN 1 85158 611 3

A catalogue record for this book is available from the British Library

Typeset in Sabon by Servis Filmsetting Ltd, Manchester

Printed in Great Britain by BPCC Wheatons, Exeter

# Contents

# Acknowledgments

AS USUAL, I did not do this on my own. The following people were also involved, either by providing information or just listening: Russell Kyle of the Glasgow *Evening Times*; Stephen Wilkie and Mark Sweeney of the Scottish *Sun*; James Freeman of the *Herald*; Ian Kellagher of BBC Scotland; Audrey Gillen and James Rougvie of the *Scotsman*; freelance journalist Dougie Miller; and Mrs Effie Drummond, Alastair Stirling, Michael Strathern, David Coutts, John Conway, Adam Hay and Janet Newman of the Missing Persons Bureau. Thanks are also due to Martin Jones for his advice, John Carroll for his help, Stanley Leech for the photography, and my wife, Margaret, for listening. Grateful appreciation is also extended to those others who asked not to be named and to Bill Campbell of Mainstream who suggested the book in the first place. Without the help of all these people, it would not have happened.

# Introduction

CRIME DETECTION SEEMS very easy on television. Everything is very neat, everything explained, with all the loose ends tied up in a nice knot in time for *News at Ten*. More often than not, the murderer is unmasked by a sleuth armed with at least one quirk which helps him get his man. Morse has his opera and brilliant analytical mind, Poirot has his schoolboy Belgian and little grey cells, Fitz has psychological insights which border on the supernatural, while Taggart has to make do with a scowl and a gruff line in street patter. That, and a scriptwriter working with the sure knowledge that the killer will be caught. There is seldom, heaven forbid, any danger of an unsolved case in most detective series.

The problem with real life is that it is not neat. Murderers don't often plot their crimes with military precision, as in Agatha Christie novels. Sometimes, they don't even know their victim and the crime is a spur of the moment thing, impulsive, random, undetectable. And the police officers trying to catch them are just ordinary people like the rest of us, doing a job. And don't let any of them tell you anything different.

There are good cops and bad cops and even ugly cops. There are those who care and those who couldn't care less. There are those who love what they do and those who loathe it. But the one thing they all – *all* – have in common is that they can make mistakes. They are, after all, only human.

In real life the villain can get away with his or her crime, some to offend another day, others to slide into obscurity. Not every crime can be solved, despite what politicians like to think. Sometimes a mistake has been made by the investigating officers. Often there simply is not enough evidence to link a particular offence with a particular person.

In the following pages you will find 13 cases of unsolved murder, one missing person case which may turn out yet to be murder, one suicide which could have been murder and one solved murder with some unanswered questions attached. With the exception of this last case and the alleged suicide, they are all technically still on police books. At the time of writing there seems to be no hope of a solution but it is possible that for some of them one vital clue could be unearthed and the killer caught. Stranger things have happened.

Unsolved cases are particularly distressing to relatives of the victim. Many of them cannot properly get on with their lives because of the questions remaining over the loss of their loved one. The initial senseless and often brutal act continues to haunt and affect them forever afterwards. Mothers weep in the night, wondering why it was their child that was taken. They cannot grieve properly, sometimes becoming bitter and angry and even afraid. They cannot stand the thought that the killer is still walking around free, while their son or daughter or wife or husband or lover is dead.

Murderers cannot work in a vacuum. Someone knows who they are. Someone knows what they have done. And that someone helps cover it up, either literally, by assisting in the disposal of the body or lying to the police and providing an alibi, or figuratively, by pretending nothing has happened, by ignoring the nagging doubts in their own mind: where was he that night? Why did he have blood on his clothing? Where did he get that scratch?

This is not an exhaustive collection of unsolved cases in Scotland. Naturally, there are others. Neither are there cases of not proven here: whatever you may think of the verdict, it does mean the accused is acquitted and the case is officially unsolved. But there has been so much controversy over this unique Scottish verdict that a fuller examination of certain cases will have to wait.

Here then are cases for which there is no final solution, cases where the real killer must remain a shadowy figure stalking the alleyways of our imagination. Perhaps temporarily, perhaps forever.

*Douglas Skelton,*
*November 1993*

# The Little Girl Who Lived Down the Lane

EVER SINCE CRIME began, authorities the world over have faced the problem of how to identify criminals.

In the Bible it was easy: when Cain rose up to slay his brother Abel, God merely had to smite him to leave a mark on his cheek. Wherever he went after that, he would be recognised as a fratricidal killer. Perhaps using that as an example, successive cultures have developed their own marks of Cain. In order to both punish criminals and let others know exactly what sort of wrongdoers they were, eyes have been gouged, tongues slit, ears, hands and feet lopped off, flesh branded and backs flayed. Such practices were still in use in some parts of Britain until the early nineteenth century and in Russia until around 1860.

But as the human race became increasingly sophisticated and developed a more liberal conscience – some of it at least – other forms of identification had to be developed. François Eugene Vidocq, the thief-turned-detective who formed the French *Sûreté* during the early nineteenth century, insisted that his detectives regularly visit jails to view the prisoners, so that if one of the villains should cross their path again, they would know him. Over a century later, American detectives in some cities were required to attend daily line-ups at headquarters where all the felons arrested during the previous day and night were paraded to allow the officers to become familiar with them should they ever stray into their precinct.

Vidocq also initiated the first system of criminal records, with descriptions of the subjects carefully updated and kept. This spawned the pseudo-science of anthropometry which reasoned that no two individuals bore the exact same body measurements. This latter system, developed by another Frenchman, Alphonse Bertillon, in 1879, entailed the recording and storing of various personal details, such as arm and leg lengths, facial shapings, and length of fingers and feet.

Yet another early system saw felons holding their hands up just below their faces when having their police photographs taken so that the scars and abnormalities common among the so-called lower classes could be easily seen and used in future identification.

Although both these systems seemed to work, they proved too cumbersome for workable records to be kept and were gradually replaced by the new science of fingerprinting.

The theory itself – that no two persons have the same marks on the tips of their fingers – was not new. For centuries the Chinese had used thumbprints as a means of signing and sealing documents, while in the seventeenth century the Italian anatomist Marcello Malpighi first described the patterns on the fingertips. Further researches followed, with scientists continuing to study and describe the many whorls, ellipses and triangles to be found on the fingers and palms of our hands.

In the mid-nineteenth century, William Herschel, a clerk in the British Indian colony, discovered that native workers were making their mark for receipt of pay and then rejoining the end of the queue again to draw more by making another mark. Herschel decided to circumvent this systematic fraud by insisting that each worker add his fingerprints to a register. They would then 'sign' for their pay by leaving their fingerprint, which could be more easily checked. Herschel also discovered that an individual's fingerprint does not change over time. Later researchers would find they are formed in the womb during the sixth month of pregnancy.

The first crime recorded to have been solved by using fingerprints took place in Tokyo in 1879. A thief had made his getaway over a fence, leaving behind a dirty handprint. This was inspected by Scottish doctor Henry Faulds, who had been making a study of the use of handprints as a means of signature. Faulds was able to clear a suspect being held by the

Japanese authorities for the theft and subsequently prove the guilt of another man by taking his palm print and comparing it with the one left on the fence. Dr Faulds wrote of his findings in a British scientific journal, *Nature*. On reading of Fauld's work, Herschel, believing that his own theories were being stolen, launched a bitter campaign for recognition through the pages of the same publication.

Eventually, though, it was left to another scientist, Sir Francis Galton, to pull together the various strands of research and package them into an identifiable branch of science. In 1892 he wrote a book which laid down a system of classification, a technique later perfected by Sir Edward Henry, a former inspector in the Bengal Police, who in 1901 became head of Scotland Yard's new fingerprint bureau.

However, the first murder case to be solved using the new techniques was committed not in Europe, but in Argentina. In the latter half of the nineteenth century, a Croatian-born detective named Juan Vucetich, based in the town of La Plata, read articles penned by Galton and others and created his own system of fingerprint identification, or dactyloscopy as it was known. He managed to interest fellow officers in his process and in 1892 one of these men used the Vucetich fingerprinting system to prove that a mother had beaten her two children to death. She had accused a male neighbour but the detective found bloody prints on the door to the shanty in which the children were living; prints which matched those of the mother. Confronted with this evidence, she broke down and confessed. This and another murder case solved by fingerprint evidence convinced the Argentinian authorities that the theory was workable, and in 1894 the country became the first in the world to officially adopt fingerprinting as a means of criminal identification.

In 1916 the Argentinians went even further. They announced they were to set up the world's first universal register: a directory of every citizen's fingerprints. This was not only Vucetich's dream but also every other police officer's the world over, then and now. But the populace was violently opposed to the idea and after a series of riots, during which the building which was to house the central records was damaged, the scheme was abandoned. A bitter Juan Vucetich retired from public life and died in 1925, suffering from both tuberculosis and stomach cancer.

It was a full ten years after the Argentinian murder that the first European homicide, a case of homosexual jealousy in Paris, was solved using fingerprints. In that case, the killer gave himself up when he realised he had been unmasked literally by his own hands, his confession – like that of the Argentinian mother – saving the authorities the trouble of proving in court that fingerprints were indeed a useful tool in tracing murderers. However, the police and prosecutors in Britain's first fingerprint murder were not to be so lucky.

In 1905 the police arrested two petty thieves, brothers Albert and Alfred Stratton, for the brutal murders of 71-year-old shopkeeper Thomas Farrow and his wife. Officers had found a clear thumbprint, eventually found to match Alfred Stratton's on a cash box. The accused man refused to crack and confess so the Crown found itself in the unenviable position of having to prove to the jury and a somewhat sceptical judge that the 'new-fangled' system was admissible as evidence in a murder trial. The intricacies of fingerprinting were explained to the jury with the use of enlarged photographs. One jury member was also fingerprinted to help prove the theory and ultimately the brothers were found guilty and hanged.

In 1911 the US Supreme Court ruled that properly prepared fingerprint evidence was relevant and competent following a murder case in Chicago. And so, throughout the world, the techniques were established and accepted that would revolutionise crime investigation and detection.

However, fingerprinting, like any other process, is only as efficient as the men and women applying it. Criminals and civil-rights groups realise that liberties can be taken – it is easy to transpose fingerprints from one place to another if you know how – and mistakes – in preparation of specimens and identification – can be made. For instance, police have been guilty of failing to fingerprint items which would normally be expected to be tested, occasionally even the murder weapon.

In one recent Scottish murder case, certain productions were not tested because investigating officers claimed there was too much blood smeared on them. However, other experts alleged that the blood would act as a seal, effectively holding the print on to the item and they really should have been tested. In the end, the accused was found guilty but his conviction owed more to a confession – later retracted – than the quality of the police investigation, which was very poor indeed. The convicted man's appeal has since been turned down, although there remain a number of unanswered questions connected to the case – including the identity of the person who left smudged handprints at the murder scene. Also, in Scotland, the prosecution is under no obligation to disclose evidence which could assist in the defence. This means, for instance, that a host of fingerprints can be found at a locus which clearly do not match the accused's – and the Crown do not need to tell anyone. So much then for the pursuit of justice.

But it is not only our hands and fingers which can help in identification. Blood, hair and even teeth can assist, although they cannot prove identity in themselves, while more recently, genetic fingerprinting, or DNA profiling, has come to the fore, albeit controversially. And like our fingers and palms, our feet and toes also bear unique ridges and patterns. Some American hospitals have been using footprints to identify babies since 1915, while on 4 November 1952 in Glasgow, a man was convicted for the first time in Britain on the basis of a toeprint – in his case his big toe. William Gourley was found guilty of breaking into premises and trying to blow a safe, somehow managing to leave behind a clear imprint of his big toe.

But it is fingerprinting which has continued to seize the public's imagination. Techniques for finding, storing and identifying these marks of Cain have been developed and are now used by police departments in most parts of the world.

In Britain, there are problems, of course. In this country, citizens are not fingerprinted unless they have been arrested, leaving the vast majority of its citizens unclassified. Attempts to create national registers similar to the one mooted in Argentina in 1916 have also failed. The police and some politicians love the notion, claiming that innocent people have nothing to fear; the public remain unconvinced while civil-liberties groups view these moves with the mistrust of a sparrow for a cat. However, there are plans to create a national DNA register in the very near future.

In the absence of such a fingerprint register, the police find themselves stumped when a full or partial print is found at the scene of a crime and no match can be found in their records. Although it can be used later for corroborative purposes if the culprit is found, in terms of leading detectives to their quarry the print can be as much use as an ash-tray on a motorcycle.

So if the fingerprint is the only, or best, evidence available, then police may wish to take steps which will at least eliminate vast sections of the local population, if not lead them directly to the killer. And for that, they rely on the goodwill of the public. That was exactly what happened in 1952, following the brutal murder of a four-year-old child in an area of Glasgow known as Garnethill.

Garnethill is perhaps the only patch of Glasgow's city centre which still remains largely residential. Situated north of the city's most famous thoroughfare, Sauchiehall Street, and rambling towards West Graham Street over a hill so steep that even The Little Engine That Could would probably not even try, the area begins properly at Cambridge Street to the east and ends to the west at the jumble of motorway slip roads at Charing Cross.

Visually, it has not changed much since 1952. Certainly, some of the tenements have been bulldozed to make way for smart new red-brick homes. Many of the remaining buildings look cleaner now than they would have done in the austere days of post-war Britain, thanks to the passion for stone cleaning in the city during the Eighties. In one such sand-blasted tenement is the Tenement House, a National Trust for Scotland property which has won a number of top tourism awards. Tourists flock to this small flat which acts as a living museum of the way ordinary Glaswegians lived between the wars. But there have been other, more noticeable, more destructive changes. Now there are playgrounds that used to be buildings and buildings that used to be churches and although most of the streets are still there (the area has been spared many of the ravages of town planners, although not escaping them completely) they show the signs of life in the Nineties – one-way streets, residents' parking bays and the ubiquitous parking meters. However, there is still the proliferation of guest- and boarding-houses which helped give Garnethill its unique atmosphere back in the early Fifties, when it was known as the Soho or Bohemia of Glasgow. They said then that the streets never slept.

The people who live in the area have changed, of course, but it still has a cosmopolitan feeling about it, largely due to its new citizens – mostly Chinese or Far Eastern, for this is the city's Chinatown – rather than the transient population which inhabited the 'digs' of old. And then there are the art students, of course, who attend the Charles Rennie MacIntosh designed School of Art. But perhaps somewhere in the new Garnethill there is a resident who can remember the Garnethill of old. Perhaps there is someone who recalls those damp and depressing days in October 1952 when the streets, normally filled with the sound of children's laughter, fell silent, when parents held their children close and prayed for the arrest of the shadowy person who left a young child to die on a set of cold stone steps. An arrest which never came.

The last time anyone other than her killer saw four-and-a-half-year-old Betty Alexander alive for certain was as she played with friends outside her home at 43 Buccleuch Street, Garnethill. She looked happy and smart in her fawn brown coat, kilt, grey and red jersey, fair stockings and brown shoes. Her unruly curly fair hair was brushed as neat as possible, her brown eyes sparkled, her young face marred only by the small scar on the right-hand side of her forehead.

On the afternoon of Tuesday 7 October, she helped her

grandmother make the beds in the house and then went down to a local grocer to help him in his shop, something she often did. Later, she returned to her grandmother with some flowers from the shop.

'Then she went downstairs to play,' Mrs Isobel Alexander, her grandmother, later told reporters. 'She was whistling and singing. That was the last time I saw her.' She continued: 'She was a lovable, sweet little girl who used to talk to anyone who spoke to her but would not wander away of her own accord.'

But at some point, Betty did wander away from her street, although whether it was of her own volition or whether she was abducted or enticed we will never know. When she did not return home, her mother Barbara went out to find her, walking the streets and lanes, calling her daughter's name. But there was no sign of the little curly haired girl with the scar on her forehead.

A larger search-party was formed by friends and neighbours. Ultimately, the police were alerted and joined the search. Later that night, at about eight p.m., Barbara Alexander thought she heard her daughter calling to her from the lane which runs between Buccleuch Street and West Graham Street. The worried mother walked up the gas-lit alleyway, peering where she could into back courts and shadowy corners, calling out Betty's name again. But Betty did not answer and Mrs Alexander left Buccleuch Lane, her hopes dashed. She had no way of knowing that she could have walked within a few inches of where her daughter may have been lying, either dead or near to it.

By the following day the press were on the story, too. After reports in the evening and daily papers, readers contacted the police with claims that they had seen the girl in various parts of the city. Each sighting was carefully checked. None of them turned out to have been Betty Alexander.

One person even thought she had seen the child crying in Woolworths in Sauchiehall Street just before closing time on Wednesday night. The police asked the manager to re-open the store to see if the little girl had been locked in somewhere. But it, like all the others, proved to be a false alarm.

At assembly in the local primary school, the headmaster told his young charges of the child's disappearance and asked for any children to come forward who might have seen Betty or who possibly heard her calling out from the darkness of the lane. A number of youngsters came forward to the detectives at the headmaster's side with information.

The search shifted gear, extending to the entire 16 square miles covered by what was then the Northern Police Division. Detective Chief Inspector Neil Beaton admitted publicly that fears for the girl's safety were mounting. But, he said, everything possible was being done. 'Teams of police, policewomen and detectives are on special patrols,' he said, 'and we have inquired into hundreds of reports by people claiming to have seen Betty. Nothing has come to light.' By the time he made that statement, two days after the girl's disappearance, perhaps the experienced officer knew there was little hope of finding her alive.

But the search went on. The driver of a dark saloon car seen in the street on the night Betty disappeared was traced – and eliminated from inquiries. An appeal for a man said to have been seen with her was made. He was wearing a blue suit and was described as small, stout and middle aged. This man, though, was never found.

Search-parties combed old air-raid shelters, disused now but still evident in bleak post-war Britain. Dark closes and seldom-used lanes were visited many times. Parks, including nearby Kelvingrove Park, were searched and sections of the Forth and Clyde canal at Port Dundas were dragged by Ben Parsonage of the Glasgow Humane Society. But still there was no sign, not even the slightest trace, of the little girl. The girl's photograph was copied and posted on every police box and police station in the city. Police officers folded copies of the snap into their notebooks for ease of recognition on the off-chance that they came across her during a patrol.

Friends, neighbours and people who had never even met the girl threw themselves wholeheartedly into the hunt. It is at times like this that people often come together, showing a community spirit which is still seen even today when such feelings are said to be dead. Later many of these same people would come together to murmur darkly of lynchings and vigilante justice. But that was after the shock of a young girl's brutal murder turned to fear and suspicion. For now, local mothers, some of whom might not even have known the Alexanders, formed their own groups and searched the neighbouring areas of Anderston and Partick by torchlight. Their leader, Mrs Rose McGurley, a neighbour to the Alexanders, said: 'Most of these women have been neglecting their homes to help look for Betty. I've spent over 16 hours going over back courts and closes in the district and will go on looking until she is found.' But the little girl was closer to her home than the searchers realised.

At about two p.m. on Friday 10 October, Mrs Agnes Hunter, the 55-year-old cleaner at the Royal Hospital for Sick Children's dispensary in West Graham Street, went out into the building's backyard to beat carpets. She always went into the yard to do this at around that time on a Friday. No one else had any reason to go there on any other day – both the door from the dispensary and the wooden gate leading into Buccleuch Lane at the rear were kept locked. The yard was private property and nobody had been in it – not even part of the search-party – since she had last been there the Friday before. At least that's what she thought.

What she found when she opened the door from the dispensary sent her screaming back into the building. The little girl lay on her back on top of her coat at the head of a small flight of steps leading to the dispensary door. Her clothes were disarranged although there were no immediately visible signs of injury. But she was dead – and had been for some time. She may even have been lying there since the very first night she went missing. 'It was a terrible sight,' said the cleaning woman later. 'I want to forget it as quickly as possible.'

The courtyard had not been searched during the three days and two nights that Betty had been missing. There had seemed to be no need. Everybody had been looking for a little girl who was full of life and who had perhaps wandered off and got herself trapped somewhere. The courtyard was surrounded by ten-foot-high stone walls, too high for such a little girl to climb over. The gate was always locked. It was not overlooked by any houses, apart from the caretaker's house but he and his family had moved out six weeks before. Only the dark and empty windows looked down emotionlessly on the scene now. Scrawled in white paint on the wall beside the gate leading from the lane to the yard were the words 'The Wages of Sin is Death'. Hardly a fitting epitaph for a young child. But it was a message that many locals were ready to give the culprit when he – or she – was caught.

News of the horrific discovery pulsed through the neighbourhood as swiftly as it took the police to respond. Even as detectives converged on the locus and as members of Glasgow police's scientific bureau studied it for clues, locals began to gather at either end of the lane. There were about 1,000 of them, grim-faced ordinary people who strained and jostled to see past the police cordon, fearful for the safety of their own children and angry that such a thing could happen in their neighbourhood. As time passed, the faces changed but the sentiments remained the same. They stood in the chilly autumn rain, watching and waiting, each fragment of news gleaned from a talkative police officer passed backwards among the throng, like a stick floating out to sea on the tide. Uniformed officers also stood guard over the huge iron gate at the end of a passageway leading from Milton Free Church in West Graham Street into the courtyard. The public gathered there, too.

The nearest inhabited house to the murder scene was that of a 69-year-old man called William Brown. He knew Betty Alexander and had heard no screams or any noises in the lane. 'I'm often about the lane quite late at night,' he told reporters. 'It's not very well lighted but I've seen or heard nothing in the last three nights. I saw Betty myself at about five p.m. on the night she went missing. She was playing with my granddaughter.'

James Alexander, the girl's father, pale faced with anxiety and with deep dark circles around his eyes from lack of sleep, was called to the dispensary to identify his daughter's body.

Later, the man, who worked in Glasgow's meat market, would offer everything he owned to anyone who could help find his daughter's killer. But everything he owned was not enough.

It was the most intensive inquiry the city had ever seen. The death of such a young child – according to police spokesmen the first of its type in Glasgow for 30 years – had horrified the city. Police officers were drafted in from other divisions until there was an initial team of 2,000 uniformed officers and 120 detectives. Members of the scientific bureau went over the locus with a fine toothcomb, searching desperately for clues which could lead them to the killer. The wrought-iron gate was taken down from its hinges and taken away to headquarters for examination, as was the wooden gate leading to the lane. In those days, fingerprints were not lifted at the scene of the crime but photographed at the locus, since it was believed, wrongly, that lifting them – generally by dusting them and removing them using adhesive tape – could destroy any possible evidential value. On occasion, the source of the latent print would be taken to the laboratory, as in this case. Eventually, that wooden gate would yield the only real clue in the case. The girl's clothes were taken away to be thoroughly scrutinised for any traces of the killer. Fragments of the stone steps on which she lay were also taken away for study.

A police Alsatian named Skipper was borrowed from the Renfrewshire force. The dog was taken to the locus and given some of the child's clothes not being subjected to forensic examination before being sent off to trace her scent. But the dog was unable to pick up a trail and this particular line of inquiry was closed.

Detectives leading the hunt believed the killer may well have been local. They felt that only a local person would have known the yard was safe from the prying eyes of others. But they could not be sure. At the same time, they were aware that rumours were sweeping the streets of the area with the rain that was still falling steadily and they knew it would only take one small incident to tip the locals over the edge. 'There is no particular man being sought,' said Chief Superintendent McIlwrick, pointedly, trying to defuse the atmosphere of fear and suspicion. 'In fact, we cannot even be certain at the moment that it was a man. No possibility is being overlooked.'

But the press was already certain that the killer was male. That assumption would later be confirmed by police when it was announced that the girl had been suffocated and 'criminally assaulted'. Newspapers said her body had been 'outraged'. We call it sexually assaulted.

Meanwhile, the area was flooded with officers conducting door-to-door inquiries. Vast numbers of people offered to give voluntary statements. Slowly, the police built up a table of the girl's movements up to about half past five on the Tuesday night. She had been seen in Rose Street and her mother said she heard the pitiful cries of 'Mummy, Mummy' in the lane at about eight p.m. Three other young girls had also heard the voice, which they were certain was Betty's. A dozen youngsters, accompanied by their parents, were asked to attend Northern Division headquarters in Maitland Street to help detectives build up a fairly accurate picture of the girl's movements on to about six p.m. Eventually, their timetable would be extended to seven p.m. But it was not enough. None of it was enough.

Part of Garnethill was at that time the city's bedsit land, populated by a constantly changing stream of transients, drifters, salesmen and seasonal workers. The police managed to speak to most of the people on the guest-house owners' books but some of them proved elusive, thus hampering investigations. However, by Monday 13 October police officers had spoken to almost 4,000 people in connection with the murder. These statements would be checked and rechecked by detectives, growing more desperate for something which would lead them to the murderer. Each line was carefully scrutinised in the hope that one would yield up even the tiniest clue. They even contacted mental institutions around the city to see if any of their patients had been released or escaped.

Meanwhile, detectives searched the caretaker's house, the only house overlooking the courtyard. It had been empty for six weeks and the searchers found nothing of any value there. However, the fact that the caretaker and his family had left the house long before the murder was not enough for the rumour-mongers. Both he and old Mr Brown would soon be subjected to a barrage of accusations and vicious rumour. The hate campaign became so intensive that they were eventually forced to report it to the police, who issued a stern reminder to the public that these men were not under suspicion.

Betty Alexander was buried in Cadder cemetery to the north of the city on Monday 13 October. The service itself, led by three clergymen, was held in her home and the cortège was due to move solemnly through the streets to the cemetery. As the little white coffin was carried from the closemouth by James Alexander and three male relatives, two senior police-men in uniform standing on the pavement came to attention and saluted.

Over 5,000 people stood silently in the streets to watch the procession go past, bringing traffic to a standstill. Many of them were from other parts of the city, for the death of the little girl had touched all of Glasgow. Some of them had gath-ered there four hours before the mourners were due to leave the house. They lined the route, four or five deep, waiting in the gentle rain for the procession to pass. They were mostly women, many dabbing their eyes with handkerchiefs, two fainting and having to be carried away by police officers. And then there were the children, saying their last farewell to their friend. But there were a few men also, their hats doffed, their faces stiff as they struggled against the emotion of the moment.

A handful of family and friends clustered round the grave-side as the coffin was lowered into the ground. There were more than 50 wreaths, bouquets of flowers and memorial vases from people all over Glasgow on the ground beside them. There was also a floral cross, made up of chrysanthe-mums and anemones, bearing the card: 'To Bunkum – our dear wee Betty, from Daddy and Mummy'.

It was during the funeral that the crowd turned into a mob. There had already been signs of their feelings when a new rumour sprinted around the streets that a man had been arrested and was being held in Maitland Street. It was not true but the crowd that gathered around the police station did not know that and officers had to disperse them.

But then, as the funeral procession made its way to Cadder, a woman tried to abduct a young boy and the crowd's anger grew to fever pitch. The 15-month-old boy had been picked up and carried away from the door of a shop where his mother was shopping. An aunt of the youngster saw the woman with the boy and challenged her. She wrestled the child from the woman's grasp and the police were called. News of what the woman had attempted was soon communicated to the crowd who had earlier watched the small coffin go by on its way north. Luckily, the police reached the woman before they did, but this did not stop them from surrounding the police van with cries of 'lynch her'. Finally, the van managed to push its way through the mob and the woman was later charged with plagium, or child-stealing.

Then came news of a twist in the hunt, a twist then quite unique in Scottish law. Experts had found a latent fingerprint on the wooden door taken from Buccleuch Lane. Although police believed that the killer had entered the courtyard via the passageway from West Graham Street, he must obviously at one point have touched the door. It was, however, only a partial print, which is difficult to match at the best of times. Police records were checked to try and find such a match but the owner of the prints was obviously not a known criminal. Clearly, other steps had to be taken. The print, after all, was the only real clue they had apart from vague sightings. So, on Tuesday 14 October, the police made their dramatic announcement: every male over 17 years of age in the area was going to be asked to agree to be fingerprinted in a bid to trace the killer.

'We are investigating the possibility of trying to connect up part of a fingerprint which had been found in the vicinity of where the body was found,' said Chief Superintendent

Gilbert McIlwrick of Northern CID. 'With that end in view we are asking for the co-operation of all males in the vicinity in letting their fingerprints be taken.' This was the first time in Scotland that such a move had been taken, although the use of fingerprints in criminal identification and detection was, of course, not new.

It was not, however, the first exercise in mass fingerprinting to be undertaken in Britain. Early on the morning of Saturday 15 May, 1948, young June Anne Devaney was removed from the children's ward of Blackburn's Queen's Park hospital. Her empty cot was discovered by the duty nurse making her rounds and the child was found 300 yards from the hospital, sexually assaulted and battered to death.

But the killer made the mistake of moving a bottle before he lifted the child from the cot and detectives were able to lift a number of sets of fingerprints from it. The police traced and eliminated not only present staff but also anyone who may have been in the ward over the previous two years. Within one month of the murder they had made 642 fingerprint tests, eliminating all but one set of prints – without a doubt the killer's.

To catch him, the investigating officers decided to take fingerprint samples from every male in the Blackburn area. It was a task unprecedented in Britain and about 46,500 prints were taken. Some 200 men had been missed in the first mammoth task and so police had to cross-reference their records with the release of ration books to the area.

Three months after the murder of Anne Devaney, a match was found, that of Peter Griffiths who apparently said to officers when being arrested: 'I hope I get what I deserve.' He was found guilty of murder and hanged. After that, all the fingerprints gathered during the inquiry were publicly destroyed. Fingerprint records of innocent people are not stored in this country.

The same assurance that all records would be destroyed was made by Glasgow's Chief Constable Malcolm McCulloch in the Betty Alexander case. His statement, sent to

28

men in the area and also reprinted in the press, read as follows:

> To assist in the investigation of the crime, the Chief Constable appeals to you as a male of 17 years of age or over to allow your fingerprints to be taken. It is to be clearly understood that you may refuse to have your fingerprints taken, but nevertheless the Chief Constable hopes that he will have your full co-operation and gives you an undertaking that these fingerprints will only be used in connection with this inquiry and will be destroyed as soon as they have served their purpose.

By the following day, over 800 sets of fingerprints had been taken, while specially detailed officers began the laborious task of comparing them with the partial print found on the gate. No match would be found, even though fingerprint cards continued to flood in.

Meanwhile, the case was attracting the usual amount of attention from the city's cranks. Early on the morning of Thursday 16 October, distinctive black police cars converged on a telephone box at the junction of Peat Road and Cowglen Road on the south side of the city. The officers were responding to a call from a man who had phoned police confessing to the murder. The man was detained and taken to police headquarters where he was questioned personally by Chief Superintendent McIlwrick. But, as usual, it proved to be a false alarm. 'I do not think this man has any real connection with the murder,' said the detective, 'but of course we must question him in the hope that he might be able to help the investigation.'

But the man did not, it seems. However, that night, the people of Garnethill noticed a flurry of activity by police. Several persons were asked to call into Maitland Street police station to answer questions. But all the officers in charge of the case would say was that they were following a 'definite line of inquiry'.

The activity included visits to the police office by the chief constable, two assistant chief constables, the procurator fiscal for Glasgow, Mr Robert MacDonald, and his deputy. Professor John Glaister, the pathologist who had conducted the post-mortem, was also seen to enter the police office.

Earlier that day, police had called at a house in Buccleuch Lane not far from where the girl had been found. Members of the scientific bureau had searched both that house and a cellar next door, leaving with a number of parcels. Uniformed officers were left on duty outside the house, prompting speculation that someone had been arrested.

Then word got out that a husband, wife and their son had been detained in their home in Garnethill and taken to the police office for questioning. They were held there for 13 hours. During that time, the angry mob returned to Maitland Street, baying for blood. At one point police officers had to jam a baton into the handles of double swing doors at the main entrance to keep them out. Meanwhile, detectives were assuring the crowd – and the general public – the family had not been arrested and no charges had been preferred. All three had co-operated fully with the police in every possible way. Despite that assurance, the family had to be taken out of the police station through a side entrance to avoid the waiting crowd outside and escorted home, where another mob had gathered. They, too, were moved on by police.

The following day, checks were made on other houses in the area. The reason for the searches was never disclosed. These searches, and the intense activity of the night before, were put down to routine.

Other inquiries continued. The police traced a man who had been seen running near Buccleuch Lane shortly after the girl's body was found. He was interviewed but was able to give a satisfactory explanation of his actions. They also contacted the St Andrew's Ambulance in an attempt to trace an ambulance seen at the Sick Children's dispensary in West Graham Street on the night Betty Alexander went missing. It had been spotted by Mrs Alexander and a friend while they were searching for Betty. They saw a man standing beside his vehicle with a child wrapped in a blanket in his arms. At the time, Mrs Alexander said to her friend: 'Look, there's another wee kiddie – and us looking for Betty.'

But there was no record of an ambulance being in West Graham Street that night. The police publicly surmised that the ambulance had either come from outside the city and the driver had mistakenly gone to the dispensary instead of the Sick Children's hospital proper in Yorkhill, or that an ambulance driver was making an 'unofficial' run and was unwilling to come forward in case he found himself in trouble with his bosses. Later, Mrs Alexander conceded that it might have been a brown van she saw. Such a van was never traced.

Meanwhile, forensic officers had discovered dog hairs on Betty's clothes. Although the hairs were black there were traces of white at the ends and detectives resumed their house-to-house search, this time to look for such a dog. When they traced it, they discovered that Betty had patted the animal shortly before she disappeared.

But there were mysteries which were not so easily solved. For instance, why were the girl's shoes and socks soaking wet when they found her – yet her clothes were bone dry? And why was a shiny chrome pin she had been wearing on her kilt changed for another one? 'On the Tuesday, her grannie put a nice wee chrome pin in her kilt,' said Barbara Alexander. 'Yet when she was found dead there was a big brassy-looking pin in its place.' None of the girl's family had seen the pin before, so who had put it there?

Not one of the males asked for fingerprints had refused and the exercise had not turned up a match for the partial print found on the wooden door, so detectives decided to extend the catchment area to men who worked in Garnethill but did not live there. This included the workers in a joinery shop in Buccleuch Lane and the church officer of Milton Free Church, who had been on duty that night. Detectives also fingerprinted some of the church congregation who had been painting the railings on West Graham Street.

Officers also visited the offices of the *Daily Record* armed with a two-inch-square cutting found on the girl's body. The cutting was from a story in the sports section and, with the newspaper staff's help, they managed to track down the particular edition and where it was circulated. But that was all. The cutting, like everything else, led them nowhere.

Another lead which fizzled out took two senior detectives to Inverness to interview a man who had left his lodgings in Gartnethill suddenly on 8 October, the day after Betty Alexander disappeared. But the man was able to give them a satisfactory explanation for his move and the detectives returned south, no further forward.

After that, the inquiry slowly lost its momentum. The team had already been whittled down, first to 40 officers and then to only a handful. No new evidence was to be uncovered and newspaper interest switched to new, more pressing, subjects like the scandalous Derek Bentley case in London, the US presidential elections, the succession of knife- and razor-wielding thugs in Glasgow 'copping a Carmont' – stiff penalties from judge Lord Carmont – and whether or not the coronation of Queen Elizabeth II would be televised in Scotland. Other crimes took up police time and the case of Betty Alexander was put, figuratively speaking, into the drawer marked 'unsolved'.

Scottish police would have somewhat better luck 25 years later, when they fingerprinted the entire adult population of an Ayrshire seaside town. On 20 December 1977, Girvan café owner Enrico Iannerelli, known to locals as 'Papa Rico', was found stabbed in his café, the Derby in Dalrymple Street. A substantial amount of cash was also taken, as well as a little black book, said in court to be the victim's 'tick book'. The suggestion was made that he was a money lender and the book contained details of his clients. However, it may just have been a record of customers to whom he had given credit.

Detectives found a series of bloody fingerprints on a storeroom inside the café. Finding no match in their records, they decided to fingerprint the entire town. Eventually, they found a match for one of the prints and 48-year-old Margaret Foote stood trial in the High Court at Ayr. The woman, who had once worked for the dead man, was jailed for life. Two others who had been arrested on the same charge were freed through lack of evidence. However, detectives were unable to trace the owners of five other bloody prints found at the locus, or find the little black book. A mysterious scarred man who had been in possession of bloodstained banknotes some time after the murder also remained unidentified.

Back in Garnethill after the heat of the murder hunt died, life gradually returned to normal. Children once again began to play in the streets and forgot all about a little girl called Betty who lived and died there. Eventually, the dispensary building became part of the University of Glasgow's Department of Clinical Studies and much of the courtyard disappeared under a modern extension. But the passageway between the old building and what was Milton Free Church is still there, blocked off now by a large green wooden door topped by rolls of barbed wire. And in the lane, the building that was once the caretaker's house is also still there.

We do not know who killed little Betty. We do not know whether it was a man acting alone or with an accomplice. We do not know for sure how he got Betty's body into the courtyard, or even why he picked that particular spot to leave her. It could be that she was still alive – hence the plaintive cries heard by her mother – and he panicked after he had assaulted her, taking her to the dispensary where he believed she would be found and treated. But she was not found until it was too late.

Betty Alexander is now just a memory, a face on yellowing newsprint, a name on a white marble headstone in a cemetery. Her killer, meanwhile, has quite possibly taken his secret to his own grave.

# The Vanishing

THEY DISAPPEARED ONE cold and wet night in November 1976. Woman and child, mother and son, vanishing without a trace from the busiest road in the Highlands. They left behind a blazing car and a host of questions; questions which burn just as brightly now, almost 20 years later.

What happened to Christine Catherine Macrae, known as Renee to her friends, and her three-year-old son, Andrew David? Where were they going when they left their comfortable Inverness bungalow on Friday, 12 November 1976? What happened to them as they made their way south on the A9? Did they meet someone? And if so, who? And if that person killed them, where are the bodies?

The massive hunt for Mrs Macrae and her son covered hundreds of square miles, at its height utilising six search teams, mechanical diggers, huge water pumps, sophisticated underwater cameras, crack divers, an RAF spy plane, tracker dogs, psychics, a hypnotist and thousands of man-hours. Ostensibly, the police were treating the case as that of a missing person, but the scale of the inquiry from early on was obviously that of a murder hunt: everything that could be done was done; every stone was turned, every avenue explored, every nook and cranny investigated. But still the solution to what is Scotland's most famous mystery remained tantalisingly out of their grasp. Finally, in June 1992, Inverness police officially declared the case a double murder.

The case is still open. Sightings and information continue to come into Northern Police headquarters in Inverness. Each new CID chief has to make himself fully acquainted with the massive Macrae file. It cannot be an easy task. There are hundreds, if not thousands, of pages: statements, reports, test results, newspaper clippings, interviews. All have to be read and digested, just in case that one last, vital piece of information comes in to complete the mysterious mosaic.

It started off quietly, as most things do. Mrs Macrae, a petite, attractive blonde, told friends that she and her son, Andrew, were going south to Kilmarnock to visit her sister on that particular weekend. She also told her estranged husband, Gordon, the same story and he had no reason to disbelieve her. She kept in regular contact with her sister and often went away for the weekend. However, Mrs Macrae had told her closest friend another story. But that would not come out until later.

Mrs Macrae lived in a comfortable, six-bedroom bungalow in Cradlehill Park, Westhill, near Inverness. The house had been built by her husband's profitable building firm, Hugh Macrae and Son, which he ran with his brother, Charles. The brothers had built the firm up steadily over ten years until it was one of the biggest private house construction firms in the north of Scotland. But the couple had not lived together for some months, with Mr Macrae still staying at their old home in Drummond Crescent, Inverness.

They had remained firm friends, however, and on that Friday afternoon Mr Macrae spoke to his wife on the telephone. Knowing she did not like driving very much – and driving at night not at all – he suggested that she take the train to Kilmarnock. She told him she would be alright in the car. She was wrong. Just after four p.m. that Friday, Renee Macrae drove off in her blue-grey BMW saloon car. As far as was known in the early stages of the inquiry, that was the last time she was seen.

At ten p.m. that night, a bus driver was driving along the A9 at Dalmagarry Bridge, about 12 miles south of Inverness, when he caught sight of flames leaping up from a lay-by behind an embankment at the side of the road. He stopped his vehicle and went to investigate, finding the blue BMW on fire. There was no sign of anyone inside. By the time the fire brigade arrived, the car had been reduced to little more than a shell. And so the mystery began.

The police noted the strange incident but could not do

much at this stage. There were no signs of foul play and Mrs Macrae may have changed her mind and taken the train after all, parking her BMW in Inverness town centre from where it could have been stolen. The thieves could have driven it around before deciding to set it on fire in the lay-by. When Mr Macrae was contacted by the police about the car, he phoned his sister-in-law in Kilmarnock to learn that Renee had not, in fact, arranged to visit that weekend. There was a slight twinge of alarm then but he reasoned that he and his wife were separated, after all, and perhaps she had other plans for that weekend, plans which she did not want him to know about. As it turned out, that may not have been far from the truth.

But by Monday he began to worry in earnest. The couple's eldest son, Gordon, aged nine, had spent the weekend at his aunt's home and Renee Macrae had arranged to pick him up from school on Monday afternoon at three o'clock. She did not show up.

The police moved quickly then. In any major investigation the first 24 to 48 hours are the most important – and this trail was already three days old. The car was examined by forensic scientists in Aberdeen but the flames had destroyed any hope of finding anything useful. There was no trace inside of the clothes it was known Mrs Macrae had taken with her, or the bag they were packed in. Also missing, apparently – although not discovered until much later – was the blue pushchair she used to wheel Andrew around. She had been seen at midday in Inverness with the buggy. Portable generators were set up in the lay-by to allow teams of officers to conduct floodlit searches of the immediate area. Other officers combed the heather on the nearby hills, looking for traces of the missing woman and her child.

But they had no evidence to suspect anything other than a missing person. Chief Constable Donald Henderson told reporters that although the car added to the strangeness of the case 'there is no reason or evidence for us to suspect foul play. But I want to emphasise the concern we feel.'

Detective Superintendent John Cameron, head of

Northern CID, said there seemed to be no reason for Mrs Macrae to disappear. 'The people who saw her last tend to differ,' he said. 'Some say she was a little anxious, others say not. On average there appears to be no reason for her going off.'

What they did not say at that time was that the forensic team had found one small but possibly important clue in the boot of the car: traces of blood which matched the blood type of both Mrs Macrae and her three-year-old son. However, there was no way of knowing if these were old stains, left there after some innocuous accident, or if it was indeed evidence of violence on the night they disappeared. They also did not know of the missing woman's four-year secret.

By the following week, while the biggest search ever organised in the Highlands was in full swing, Gordon Macrae, who had managed to keep the news of his mother's disappearance from his other son, told reporters that he feared his wife and son had been murdered. Over 140 men were conducting house-to-house inquiries in the Westhill area or stretched out in blue-serge lines on the rough ground seven miles on either side of the road near Dalmagarry and had found no sign of them.

'I still cling to a slim hope that they are alive,' said Mr Macrae 'But it's only a very slim hope now. A burnt-out car, not a word from her or anyone seeing her, and knowing Renee she would have let someone know what was happening – it all makes you think she must be dead and if she is dead, she must have been murdered.'

Mr Macrae was speaking after the police had been told by Renee's closest friend of the missing woman's secret – that she had been having a four-year-long affair with a married family friend who, it was later claimed, was the missing youngster's natural father. Mrs Macrae had told her friend that she had been planning to go away with the man that weekend. The man, accountant William McDowell, was the company secretary of Gordon Macrae's building firm. He confirmed that there had been a 'tentative' arrangement to meet that weekend, but only that. The details had never been confirmed and no firm arrangements made. As soon as the news of his affair with Mrs Macrae broke, he was sacked from Hugh Macrae and Son. His wife announced she was sticking by him.

Gordon Macrae said he was 'shattered' by the news of his wife's affair. 'Although we were apart and we had our difficulties,' Mr Macrae continued, 'we were very good friends. I thought the world of her. She was a wonderful person and mother. She was one of the best. Renee would never commit suicide and she would certainly never harm her child. I am sure the police will get to the bottom of it.'

The police were doing their very best to do just that and their inquiries were beginning to bring results. They had discovered that Renee Macrae had been seen on a number of occasions in the company of a man with a zapata moustache, a drooping moustache then in vogue. The man, estimated to be between 20 and 40, had been seen in her car with her in Inverness during the ten days before she vanished. The police appealed to anyone who may have seen or talked to Mrs Macrae in that period to come forward, issuing a photofit picture of the man to help jog memories. 'There may be some small remark which didn't seem significant to them but could mean a lot to us,' said a senior detective. They later discovered that this man was seen with her on the day she disappeared.

There was another man the police desperately wanted to talk to. He was spotted on a little-used side-road running from Dalmagarry to Shennachie at eight p.m. standing half-seen in the autumn darkness and heavy rain beside a car. The side-road was about two to three hundred yards from the lay-by where the BMW was found ablaze two hours later.

Chief Superintendent John Cameron said that it was 'absolutely fundamental' to their inquiry that these men be traced. But despite repeated pleas, and the establishment of a special confidential telephone line which attracted thousands of calls, they were never found.

Concern grew with each passing day. Mr Macrae put up a reward of £1,000 for information while the investigating and search teams swelled to 400 police and volunteers, covering 100 square miles of frozen heather, forest and bracken. Two helicopters swept over the stretches of land which were difficult for the ground teams to reach. Seven frogmen from Central Police braved the waters of rivers, lochs, pools and streams. The intense cold they encountered caused three of them to take ill, but their colleagues worked on.

The hunt had caught the imagination and sympathy of people from all walks of life. In the six search teams housewives rubbed shoulders with company directors, schoolchildren with army officers. There were also students from an outward-bound school in Morayshire, who had left before dawn to reach Inverness to take part in the hunt. Meanwhile, two local firms supplied the teams with free lunches.

Then William McDowell told reporters that he had received coded telephone calls which could have been from Mrs Macrae after she disappeared. He explained that he and Renee had used special ring codes when phoning so that they would know the other was trying to get in contact – and he said that he had received two such calls, first on the weekend after she vanished and then again the following Friday. He said it might have been a coincidence, but there was always the possibility that the calls were from her. He also claimed that police officers were present when the second call was received.

He repeated that he had not arranged to meet Renee Macrae that weekend, or to stay in a Perthshire hotel with her. He later denied that there had been a plan for the two of them to go away together and build a new life. When the police discovered that the blue-hooded push-chair was missing they theorised that she may have decided to go away that weekend by herself and issued an appeal to anyone who may have seen a woman with such a push-chair at any railway station between Inverness and Perth. But no one answered the call.

Then, ten days into the inquiry, the police received information that dramatically altered the focus of their investigation. Until then, they had believed that the last time the mother and her son had been seen was around four p.m. at their home. But a young woman now said she had seen her at the premises owned by her husband's firm between 4.35 and five p.m., just as most of the staff were leaving work for the weekend.

The police moved in to quiz the firm's 700 employees, even searching its industrial incinerator for traces of bodies, while other officers continued their inquiries in Westhill. By this time, 60 houses had been searched while the floorboards of the Macrae bungalow were torn up. The police had found what they called 'clear signs' that the woman had been planning to leave for good. Clothes were packed, bedclothes stacked, toys neatly piled as if awaiting storage. Furniture had been dismantled and laid against a wall. And there was a birthday card from Renee to her son, reading: 'To Andrew, with lots of love and kisses from Mummy'. There were six kisses. The bungalow was sold in 1977.

With assistance now being requested from the Scottish Crime Squad, the search bore all the hallmarks of a major crime inquiry – still without evidence of a major crime. But seasoned detectives had their suspicions. They felt neither Mrs Macrae nor her son were going to turn up. Not alive, at any rate.

But they could not announce that officially – and would not do so for 16 years. Instead they spoke of the complications they faced in tracing the woman and her child. The blazing car was one, they said, while the lies told by the missing woman concerning her weekend plans were another. 'One of the difficulties we have here is that there was a clandestine relationship involving the missing woman and in this situation people tell little white lies,' said Chief Constable Donald Henderson. 'We have been wading through a sea of deceit and untruthfulness.'

Gradually, though, they built up a possible timetable of Mrs Macrae's final movements. At four p.m. she was seen by workmen at her home. At half past four, she was spotted at the premises of her husband's firm. Half an hour later, she was driving south on the outskirts of Inverness. A car similar to her BMW was seen at seven p.m. in a lay-by eight miles south of Inverness. After that, although there was an unconfirmed sighting of a man, woman and child in yet another lay-by, there was nothing until the car was found on fire at ten p.m. On Wednesday, 24 November 1976, a noticeably strained Cynthia Macrae, Renee's sister-in-law, took part in a reconstruction of these movements, wearing similar clothes to those now known to have been worn by the missing woman and driving a similar car.

By now the search was costing £60,000 a day and the police seemed to be learning very little. They found the maps they were using for the ground search were incorrect, with much of the land they were expected to cover too rough to be properly searched so they called on RAF Strike Command to lend a hand – and a spy plane. The Canberra aircraft was fitted with infra-red cameras and the plan was to fly over the search area for 15 miles on either side of the A9. The move confirmed to reporters that police now feared Mrs Macrae and young Andrew were dead.

And while technicians from BMW investigated the remains of the car to try and establish if the fire was caused by an engine fault, the supernatural came into play. Mrs Winifred Cary, the wife of a retired RAF wing commander and a water diviner, used her paraphernalia to opine that Renee Macrae was in the oft-searched Dalmaggary area. She held her pendulum over a map of the area and looked at a picture of the missing woman. When the pendulum swung over Dalmagarry the diviner experienced a strong reaction. The police searched the vicinity again but found nothing. Later, Swiss clairvoyant Edgar Devaux said he had received vibrations from a section of roadway four miles north of the layby where the car was found on fire. Again the area was searched, again with no results. The police would have a further brush with the spirit world during a dramatic turn of events almost one year after the Macraes first vanished.

But before that, they sent copies of a new poster all over the country, complete with clearer photographs of the missing persons, a map of the area and text urging anyone who either recognised the faces or were in the area at the time of their disappearance to come forward. In May 1977, Lancashire police loaned the team two specially trained 'body' dogs, labrador Dorrie and Bob, a German shepherd, to bring their own particular talents to bear on the thousands of acres of forest in the search area. The dogs had first been used in Lancashire during the Moors murder investigation and had then gone on to be used to great effect in the aftermath of the Six Day War, finding bodies buried up to 12 feet in the sands of the Sinai Desert. But, like the ground teams, the helicopters, the spy plane and the psychics, they could find no trace of the missing Macraes.

During the summer of 1977 little progress was made. Detectives continued to sift through the hundreds of statements and follow up information received. But they came no closer to finding Renee and Andrew Macrae and the story gradually slipped off the pages of newspapers and out of the minds of the public at large.

Then, in October, an underwater camera revealed what seemed to be a highly sinister image under 40 feet of dark, foetid water. The police had been using the camera and its operators, on loan from a Buckie company which specialised in underwater surveys for the oil industry, to probe two abandoned and water-filled quarries on the edge of Culloden Moor. The highly sensitive equipment, worth £22,000, was specially designed to operate in darkness and at great depth. Although the largest pool was only 40 feet deep, the amount of debris and litter which had been thrown into it over the years made it extremely hazardous for divers. They had previously tried dragging the bottom of the pools with grappling hooks with little success.

The camera explored the murky green depths of the quarries, uncovering the rubbish and refuse, including an entire lorry dumped in there at some time in the past. During one sweep, the operators, sitting in a boat on the surface, found a bundle, seemingly wrapped in sacking and standing upright as if weighted down. As the lens drifted past, it picked out what looked like a human face, showing the remains of eyebrows, eye sockets, a nose and a mouth gaping wide as if in a silent scream. They thought they caught a glimpse of a smaller package lying on the bottom beside it, but they could not be sure. Subsequent attempts to find them again in the almost complete darkness failed. All they had to go on was a murky five-second shot of the grisly image on videotape. Detectives studying the recording decided there was a possibility that it was what they had been searching for for almost a year. But they still hedged their bets. As Chief Constable Donald Henderson observed: 'There is a danger of seeing what you want to see.'

'We don't know with certainty what the object is,' said one detective, 'but we are definitely going to find it.'

They decided to drain the pool. An excavator, loaned by Mr Macrae's company, carved out a path to the edge of the water, allowing the large, powerful pumps to get closer.

Meanwhile, a team of top Italian divers, engaged in a search for the Loch Ness Monster for a television challenge programme, had offered to try and locate the bundle in the freezing pool. Special equipment, including a powerful lamp, to help them in their underwater quest was flown to Inverness airport from Aberdeen. The divers literally risked their lives in the treacherous pool, swimming carefully through the freezing water, picking their way between debris, finding abandoned cars, coils of barbed wire and the body of a dog wrapped in a sack. But the two bundles they most wanted to come across eluded them, their secret remaining hidden in the still, dark waters.

The draining process began, the pumps transferring 18,000 gallons of water per day into the other pool, 30 feet away. But no sooner had they started the mammoth operation than they hit a snag – the water was seeping back into the quarry almost as quickly as they pumped it out. They realised a new approach was called for: either carry the water through a series of ditches or specially laid pipes to the River Nairn half a mile away, or continue to use divers.

Part of the eight-day search was witnessed by Carol Smith, a housewife from Arbroath, who said she had been told by spirits through a ouija board about the quarry. She said when she arrived that the location was just as the spirits had described it to her. Unfortunately, the spirits could not tell the officers exactly where the bundle was.

Meanwhile, Gordon Macrae said he hoped that this was his wife's body and that the mystery would be solved. 'I'm sure my wife is dead,' he said, 'I don't think there is any question of that. If she had been alive she would have contacted someone within days of her disappearance. We were still friendly although we were living apart.'

He continued: 'I am in touch with the police every night and I feel this object in the quarry could be the end of the search. This could be what we are looking for. It has been a trying time for us and I feel the main thing now is to see justice done and to make sure no one gets away with it.'

Eventually, the police decided to abandon the idea of draining the quarry. A seven-man team of crack Royal Navy divers had arrived from Rosyth to help in the search and they were going to continue combing the bottom of the pool, assisted by the camera. Detective Chief Superintendent John Cameron, head of Northern CID, said: 'There is no other real alternative. These divers are the very best.'

And while hundreds of sightseers were held back from the immediate area by uniformed police, the divers ducked under the stinking waters. They found nothing on the first day, but on the second one of them surfaced with what appeared to be the bundle on the video tape. Excitement mounted as it was cut open. Was this going to be the end of the year-long search, the solution to the mystery that had perplexed the country?

No, it wasn't. The bundle turned out to be nothing more than garden rubbish. The hopes of the family and the police died a sad death on the lonely moor that day. The divers gave up their search, although the camera team would continue, reasoning that the things they saw could have moved during the draining process. But the following day, the entire search was called off. The police were satisfied the bundle found was the one on the tape.

It would be a further year before the search took another, more controversial, turn during which detectives would be delving not into watery deeps but the hidden recesses of the human mind. In November 1978 detectives asked witnesses in the case to volunteer to be hypnotised by a professor of psychology at an English university to see if further details could be dredged up from the depths of their subconscious. The use of such techniques was common in the USA and Australia, where in one case a witness was able to recall the registration number of a car which she was not even aware she had seen. The Israelis, meanwhile, used hypnosis in the fight against terrorism, bringing details of attacks out of witnesses' subconscious. Devon police had asked a hypnotist to help form a detailed identikit picture of a suspect in the disappearance of Genette Tate in 1978, while Inverness police themselves had utilised the technique during another murder hunt.

Out of the 21 witnesses approached, only three refused to take part. One was a woman deemed too ill, another was William McDowell. The remaining 18 provided what police called 'startling new evidence' in sessions lasting ten minutes to several hours, recorded on 18 hours of audio tape. 'We now have some very useful additional information and are re-examining everything we have learned or been told in a new light,' said Detective Inspector Donald McArthur.

Among the new information was a description of a large estate car seen in a side-road at Dalmagarry and new information regarding yet another car seen with a woman, a child and a man standing beside it several miles north of Dalmagarry. The police may have been excited by what they had learned but it took them no further.

In October 1980 Gordon Macrae was granted a divorce from his missing wife, leaving him free to marry again the following year. It is unlikely though that he will ever be able to fully put the mystery of his first wife's strange disappearance behind him. William McDowell left the Inverness area and began a new job and a new life away from the continuing glare of the media. In 1988 he was interviewed again by the police but they apparently told him nothing new, merely going over the same ground they had in 1976 and 1977.

Over the years there have been sightings from various

parts of the country. Each of them has had to be carefully checked. Each of them has proved to be groundless. In 1992 Inverness police finally admitted they viewed the mystery as a double murder. Detective Chief Superintendent George Gough, head of CID, said: 'Under the circumstances it was futile to term it a missing-persons case. We had been dealing with it since the beginning as a major investigation and we are continuing to deal with it as a major investigation. In 17 years there has been no word from Mrs Macrae, no firm sighting of her and no money withdrawn from her bank account. What we are dealing with here is a double murder.'

If that is the case, who is the killer and where did he hide the bodies? Some police believe Renee and Andrew are buried under part of the A9, then under reconstruction. This theory was investigated during the search and a digger, again borrowed from Gordon Macrae's company, was used to gouge out sections of the roadside. Nothing was found, but one detective has been reported as having caught the whiff of decomposing flesh near an earth quarry used during the reconstruction, although nothing was found. Another suggestion has been that they were still in the car when it was set on fire. However, the human body is surprisingly resilient and forensic science is sophisticated enough to find even the most minute traces. It is entirely possible that the killer took the bodies miles away from the A9, Inverness, Dalmagarry and the other places which acted as centres for the massive hunt. There are many wild places in the Highlands where bodies could be hidden and perhaps never found, except by wild animals, many remote lochs where they could be dumped.

Despite the passage of time, the police still hope to find some trace of their bodies. Apart from the fact that the discovery could put the evidence they have in a new light, it is not just a matter of trying to bring the killer to justice. 'We have a duty to find their remains,' said George Gough, 'if only so that they can be given a decent burial.' Until that day – if it ever comes – all we can do is wait.

# The Evil That Men Do

BETWEEN AUGUST AND December 1977, a series of murder investigations took place in and around Glasgow and Edinburgh. There were five victims, each of them female and each of them found in lonely places, strangled, stabbed or battered to death.

The two Edinburgh killings were undoubtedly the work of the same man – or men. The three in Glasgow were not publicly linked until May 1979, following a fourth murder the previous November. But even then the links were not definite. All the police would say was that there were similarities, and naturally, they kept most of those a closely guarded secret. They still are.

But if these four brutal acts were committed by the same person – or persons – then Scotland has a forgotten serial killer. For while the debate over the true identity of Bible John returns again and again to the pages of the country's newspapers, no one seems to remember the deadly and terrifying days and nights of 1977–78.

News of Anna Kenny's disappearance first reached the eyes and ears of the general public in August 1977. The 20-year-old woman was last seen walking alone after midnight in the Townhead district of Glasgow on Friday 5 August. She and a friend had been at the Hurdy Gurdy pub where they had met two young men. At closing time, Anna said goodbye to her friend and left with one of the men to walk to George Square, where she would catch a bus to her home in the Gorbals. She did not return home nor did she turn up for work the following Monday at Scottish and Newcastle Breweries.

When her disappearance was reported to the police, they took the usual steps, tracing her final movements, managing to trace the young man with whom she had made her last walk but he said she had left him to hail a taxi at the corner of Lister Street and Baird Street in Townhead. He told them he had heard a car braking as she turned out of sight and assumed she had found herself a taxi or had been spotted by someone she knew. The police even had divers search the canal basin at Pinkston, near to where the young man last saw her. However, with nothing to go on, the hunt wound down – as these things must do eventually. Anna Kenny was an adult, after all, and as there seemed to be no evidence of foul play there was little more that could be done.

But one-and-a-half years later, her name would again seize the headlines when her remains were found in a remote part of Argyll. But by that time another three Glasgow women had died.

It was known as the local lovers' lane but at this particular time – midday – on this particular Sunday – 2 October 1977 – it was being used by a group of youngsters out bramble-picking: Langbank was an excellent place for brambles and it was possible to find a seemingly endless supply of nice, juicy fat berries. What they found was the half-naked and brutally battered body of a woman.

The schoolboys had walked under the high bridge which carries trains from Glasgow to Greenock, heading for the hollow between the tracks and a tree-covered hill. It was here that they found her, lying among the long grass and bushes opposite the entrance to the West Ferry caravan-site.

The woman's clothing was scattered among the bushes. When the police arrived, they gathered it all together and discovered that her coat, shoes and handbag were missing, along with all forms of identification. It was therefore decided to release a description of the dead woman to newspapers, in the hope that someone would recognise her. She was only five foot tall, they said, with short, possibly dyed, dark hair, grey-blue eyes, a slight cleft in her chin and teeth missing at the front.

In her Summerston home on Monday morning, Mrs

Martha McAulay spotted the item in her newspaper and immediately realised it described her daughter, Hilda, perfectly. The 36-year-old divorced mother of two had been missing since Saturday night, when she had left her Glasgow home to go out for the evening with friends. Mrs McAulay contacted the police and later that day made the agonising journey to Paisley's Royal Alexandria Infirmary to identify her daughter's body.

Hilda McAulay, whose married name was Miller, was shy and reserved and had not had any regular boyfriends since her divorce eight years before. On her last night alive, she and her three friends had gone out dancing to the Plaza ballroom on the south side of the city. They had first popped into McNee's bar beside the dance-hall for a quick drink, where she was seen at about ten p.m. talking to a thirtysomething male.

In the Plaza, she was seen to dance with a number of men, no one more than another. However, once news of her death had been made public, a woman telephoned the then *Glasgow Herald* saying that Hilda Miller had left the dance hall with a man. The woman, who refused to identify herself, rang off after giving the reporter who took the call the man's name. She had not seen them leave herself, she said, but had been given the information by a friend who was at the dance hall that night. Detectives tracked the man down and were satisfied he had nothing to do with the woman's death.

It was not the only anonymous tip-off received by the *Glasgow Herald* that week. Another woman – again anonymous – phoned the paper with the name of yet another man, saying that it had been on her conscience for years that he could have been Bible John, the shadowy killer who murdered three women in Glasgow during 1968–69 after picking them up at the Barrowland dance-hall. Again, the police checked the lead out, but again it proved fruitless. The figure of Bible John would loom again from the darkness later in the case.

In the meantime, the police were stopping drivers on the M8 motorway which changed at that time into the A8 dual carriageway at Langbank. They wanted to know if they had been travelling on that particular stretch of road on Saturday night or Sunday morning. They also wanted to trace the driver of a dark blue van, seen parked between four and six on Sunday morning with no lights on opposite the spot where the woman's body was found. And then there was a taxi driver who was possibly spotted twice in the area, first parked in a lay-by at about half past two and then again about four hours later sitting on the hard shoulder of the motorway only about one mile from the entrance to the caravan-site. The interior lights of the black cab were on and the vehicle may have broken down. Detectives were not certain if both sightings were of the same taxi. The driver of the dark van came forward and was duly eliminated from inquiries. No taxi drivers responded to the appeal.

Similar appeals for information from people who attended the Plaza on that Saturday night or who may have been in the lovers' lane in the early hours of Sunday morning met with limited success. Many of them may have been married and out for an extra-marital fling so were therefore not willing to come forward. The police assured them that all information would be treated in confidence but many were unconvinced. Meanwhile, three female police officers were selected to mix with couples at the Plaza to try and trap the killer. The three officers became known as 'Meldrum's Angels' after the television series 'Charlie's Angels' (Detective Superintendent Douglas Meldrum was the officer in charge of the investigation).

To Glasgow police it was all so sickeningly familiar. They had met with the same resistance during the Bible John inquiry. Again, many of the possible witnesses they wanted to interview were husbands out for nights with women who were not their wives, and vice versa. In that case, undercover officers who joined the dancers at the Barrowland hall became known as 'the Partick Marine Formation Dance Team'.

There were fears that Bible John was back and up to his old tricks, although the police strongly refuted this. However, they did warn that the killer might strike again. Apparently, he did just that, eight weeks later.

It was Agnes Cooney's first outing for months. The 23-year-old children's nurse and her fellow nurse Gina Barclay had left the Bellshill children's home where they worked to go flat hunting in Glasgow on the afternoon of Friday, 2 December 1977 and had then gone on to the Clada social club in Westmoreland Street, just ten minutes' walk from the Plaza ballroom. Gina's boyfriend was a member of Trampas, a band playing in the club that night, and Agnes had listened to the music and had a few drinks and then, just after midnight, said she was going home.

Her body was found the following Sunday 20 yards away from Snipe Road, near Caldercruix in Lanarkshire. A farmer out tending cattle in a nearby field found her lying on a stretch of moorland. She had died violently, obviously having struggled with her attacker – or attackers – who had finally battered and stabbed her to death. She had 26 stab wounds on her body but had not been sexually assaulted. Still on her finger was the thin gold wedding band that had belonged to her dead mother.

Her father was shown pictures of her in an attempt to formally identify her. However, he could not be sure and it became necessary to show him the actual body. It was a horrific experience for the old man. Francis Cooney had lost his wife, mother, mother-in-law and now his daughter within six years. He was devastated.

An incident room was set up in Craigie Street police office, the nearest station to both the Clada club and the Plaza. Although not officially released until much later, police suspected from the beginning that the murders of both Hilda Miller and Agnes Cooney were linked. They were also investigating possible connections to a series of brutal rapes in the city in which two young men were forcing women into the back of their car. Two men were subsequently charged by the end of the December with 13 such rapes. There seemed to be no evidence to connect them to the killings.

Detectives also travelled to Edinburgh to probe possible links with the murders of Christine Eadie and Helen Scott, of which more later. Strathclyde Police eventually stated the murder inquiries were unconnected, although their counter-parts in Edinburgh tended to keep an open mind about it.

Other officers wanted to speak to the possibly hundreds of drivers who had driven on Snipe Road that weekend, passing by the spot where Agnes's body lay unseen. They spoke to the people who had been at the Clada club. They urged anyone who had seen a woman answering Agnes's description in the Victoria Road area of Glasgow to contact them. They wanted any woman who had been accosted by a man – or men, for they strongly believed more than one person was involved – but who had not reported it to do so now. They may have held a vital clue. Her father, Francis, agreed. His daughter was a strong girl and he believed she could have dealt with just one man. There had to be two of them, he thought.

Later Mr Cooney would be the victim of a series of malicious phone calls from a Bargeddie youth. The 18-year-old was also charged with telephoning Coatbridge police station, telling them that relatives of the dead woman were also in danger. Murders bring all sorts of lunatics out of the wood-work.

Soon officers discovered that a number of suspect vehicles had been seen in the area. The first was a silver Ford Cortina Mark 2 estate car with two or three men inside. A similar car, with a registration number ending in 354G, or numbers close to that, and a taxi sign on the roof, was also seen in Snipe Road. The driver was wearing a black leather coat or jacket and had light brown, slightly wavy hair. There was a girl in the car with him. The other vehicle the police wished to trace was a white Ford Transit, seen parked near the club. The driver of this particular vehicle was traced and cleared of any involvement.

The police also believed that the victim could have been held prisoner for up to 24 hours. She may have been kept in a van or similar vehicle, an empty house or a piece of derelict property, and tortured for a time before being taken to the farmland during the hours of darkness on Saturday night or Sunday morning, where she was killed. If it had happened earlier than that the farmer would have either seen the vehicle or found the body.

After a policewoman walked over what they knew of her route since leaving the club – wearing an identical royal-blue cagoule, blue cord trousers and fawn suede boots to those worn by the murdered woman – the police discovered that Agnes had been seen at about 12.40 a.m. on the Castle Street slip road to the M8 Glasgow-to-Edinburgh motorway trying to thumb a lift home to Coatbridge. They later found out that she was a regular hitch-hiker. The police surmised that she had been picked up by a driver in Victoria or Cathcart Road and taken to the city centre. The usual appeals were made to motorists and taxi drivers with anonymity guaranteed to anyone who came forward admitting they gave the girl a lift.

Several taxi drivers from Dolphin Taxis told officers they had heard calls over the radio that night saying: 'Pick up Cooney at the Clada club, Westmoreland Street, Crosshill.' None of them could say who finally picked the fare up and the controller could not remember if a driver had blown in to confirm the pick-up. It was possible then that she was picked up either by a 'pirate', a driver from another firm or working on his own who was tuned into Dolphin's waveband and stealing their customers, or a passing motorist who was unwilling to approach the police for fear of causing a rift in his marriage. When no one came forward, police concluded she may even have walked the two-and-a-half miles to the Castle Street interchange. She could have also walked on to Alexandra Parade where there was another sighting. But even if she did finally walk to the city centre, there was still the mystery of a black cab seen near the murder scene. That driver, like the one seen near where Hilda McAulay was found, was never traced.

Roadblocks were set up on the M8, drivers being pulled into a single lane where uniformed officers asked them if they had been travelling on the motorway during the hours in question. They took thousands of statements from car, truck and taxi drivers. Each statement had to be scrutinised again and again, read and reread in the hope that it would yield a clue.

Finally, they said they wanted to talk to the driver of a Volvo F88 juggernaut seen near Castle Street around the time Agnes was hitching. Two other persons were spotted thumbing a lift in the same spot and police wanted to interview them, too. Neither the lorry driver nor the two hitchers came forward. Nor did they ever find the owners of the two Cortinas.

Then, in the second week of the inquiry, the first phone call was received. It was made to the offices of the *Daily Record* by a man who said he knew who the killer was. But he rang off before giving any further information. 'I know the killer and where he works,' the anonymous voice said. 'I don't know what to do. After all, I'm a married man with a kiddie myself . . .' Another call was made to Coatbridge police office. On both occasions, the caller said he was too frightened to say more.

The caller was urged to phone again, before the killer struck a third time because by now, the police had publicly linked the Agnes Cooney killing with that of Hilda McAulay. Detective Chief Inspector John McDougall had confirmed to reporters that both women had their hands tied behind their back, both had disappeared as they left places of entertainment to find a taxi. Both had been found in lonely spots – lovers' lanes. And both had been murdered, police believed, for sexual reasons, although Agnes Cooney at least had not been sexually assaulted. Circumstances relating to Anna Kenny's disappearance were similar. But as no body had as yet been found, the police did not publicly link her disappearance with the murders. Not yet. A soft-spoken man did eventually phone Glasgow police again but as usual rang off before detectives had time to glean any information from him.

Meanwhile, the spectre of Bible John rose again – and this time police attached some credence to the rumours by interviewing a man who had been a suspect in the 1968–69 killings. This man had been sent to the state hospital at Carstairs following a particularly brutal rape but was now free. However, this line of inquiry led nowhere.

The murder hunt eventually petered out. There were no further leads to follow, no further clues to track down, no further suspects to interview. All police could do now was wait and hope that something new would break before there was another murder. They were in for a disappointment.

Mary Gallagher's savagely beaten body was found at the foot of a 20-foot wall near a footpath crossing waste ground between Flemington Street and Edgefauld Road in Springburn almost one year later. The four-foot-11-inch teenager was discovered by a man walking across the waste ground on the morning of Monday, 19 November 1979. The 17-year-old had left her home in Endrick Street at 6.45 p.m. on Sunday night to meet two friends and then go on to the Firhill social club attached to Partick Thistle Football Club's ground in Maryhill. She had been cutting across the path to get to Avonspark Street and the home of one of her friends. When she did not turn up, her friends assumed she was not coming so went on without her. When she did not return home, her mother assumed she was staying the night with friends.

When the girl was found, she was still wearing her dark jacket, slacks and distinctive calf-length leather boots. But her handbag was missing.

The girl was the eldest of a family of six and her mother, Katherine, had to be placed under sedation when she was informed. The girl's father, divorced from her mother, was traced and also told. Later Katherine Gallagher appealed to anyone who could help to come forward. 'I hope anyone who knows this man will tell the police,' she said. 'He must be caught.'

At the time, though, police were playing down any suggestion of a link with the murders of Hilda McAulay and Agnes Cooney. That would change. Apart from saying that her death was 'extremely savage and brutal', the officer in charge of the case, Detective Chief Inspector Norman Walker, would say very little about the way the girl died. All he would say was that the man who murdered her may well have been heavily blood-stained himself and appealed for anyone who used the path on Sunday night and who may have seen either the girl or a man with blood on his clothes to let them know. Meanwhile, scene-of-crime officers scanned the muddy pathway and surrounding wasteland with metal detectors in a bid to find the murder weapon. The police would not say what they were looking for – but whatever it was, they did not find it.

Although the path was known locally as Mugger's Alley, robbery did not seem to be the motive. Her handbag was missing but it was known that the girl, who worked as a machinist with an East End firm and who earned spare cash by baby-sitting, only had a couple of pounds in her purse. The motive was sexual.

There had been a number of attacks on women walking on the path as it neared Barnhill railway station. The police said they wanted to speak to three youths who had been seen in the area as well as the driver of a dark green Jaguar seen turning into Edgefauld Place between 6.30 and seven p.m. on Sunday night.

Photographs of the girl's high-heeled boots were released, as well as a picture of a similar handbag. And, as usual, they staged a reconstruction of the girl's last known movements. The smallest policewoman on the city force was recruited and walked the murder route, from the girl's home in Endrick Street to Barnhill station, twice – once in daylight and once in darkness – in an attempt to jog memories.

And while the policewoman fulfilled her chilling duty, a woman spotted Mary Gallagher's imitation leather handbag in an Edgefauld Road closemouth and took it to the police. Almost 100 officers flooded the area, banging on doors, stopping people in the street, desperately trying to find out if anyone had seen someone drop the handbag in the close or throw it away. Someone, they felt, must have seen something. But no one, it seems, saw anyone lay the handbag down. And all the while, the police feared the killer would pounce again.

And then another 17-year-old girl was attacked on the

same footpath. Luckily, she lived to tell the tale and was able to tell the police that her attacker was a man aged around 30. Convinced this man was their killer, detectives refused to divulge any of the girl's details for fear of placing her in danger.

But they were no further forward in finding their man. Well over 2,000 people were interviewed in door-to-door inquiries which yielded very little. Of one thing they were sure, though – someone was shielding him. They continually emphasised the fact that his clothing would have been heavily blood-stained and someone must have seen him. And the handbag was placed in that close in such a way that it could not possibly have been missed. Someone wanted them to have the bag. So, unless the killer was taunting them, someone who knew what he had done must have placed it there. But who? And why would they not come forward?

These questions would never be answered. And the next chapter in the serial would reach a horrified public six months later.

Anna Kenny's makeshift grave was found by two shepherds as they worked in the area known as Rockfield, near Skipness in picturesque Argyll, on Wednesday, 23 April 1979. She had been missing for 21 months and all that was left of her was a skeleton – and traces of some form of material which had been bound around her ankles and neck.

However, the detectives first called to the scene did not know that this grisly discovery would be the final link in a murder chain stretching across the west of Scotland. One of their first thoughts was that it was a gypsy grave – travelling people often used an area near here to camp and perhaps they had just buried one of their number without bothering to tell the authorities. Then there may have been some form of black-magic connection – two years before a minister had declared the area a centre for occult practices, with devotees based in nearby Carrodale.

The only thing they had which could help them identify the body was the corpse itself – and they initially believed it was male, thanks to a local rumour that a man had been buried in this area some months before. However, this theory was quashed as soon as the medical men arrived. They could tell almost immediately that the bones were that of a woman aged between 18 and 35 years, five foot one inch to five foot three inches in height and was probably well built. Dental experts made impressions of the teeth to compare against records of missing persons from all over Scotland, including Renee Macrae, the Inverness woman who vanished with her son in November 1976 (see previous chapter).

Eventually, the body was identified as that of Anna Kenny and the material round the neck and binding the feet proved to be what was left of some red and white cloth. And when seen last, Anna Kenny had been wearing a red and white striped shirt. The girl, then, had been picked up by someone in the Townhead area and brought to this lonely place, where she was strangled, possibly raped, and buried in two feet of moist Argyll earth.

The question was, of course, who did it – and why pick this place to dump the body? 'What really stumps us is why the killer buried her here, in a place which is not only used by gypsies and tinkers but is also a well-known lovers' spot,' said one senior detective, pointing out that between Arrochar and Skipness there are many quiet and uninhabited areas of moorland where the victim could have been buried and never discovered.

And they were also being forced to consider possible links with the other three murders. 'There is nothing to show a definite connection, but there are similarities,' said one detective. Some of those similarities are as follows: Hilda McAulay, Agnes Cooney and Anna Kenny were all bound by the feet or hands and their bodies left in well-known lovers' lanes. Agnes Cooney and Anna Kenny were last seen in the Townhead area of Glasgow, Mary Gallagher was murdered less than a mile from there. Hilda McAulay may have ended up there as she made her way home to Summerston from the South Side. All the victims were picked up at the weekend. They all died violently. With the exception of Mary Gallagher, they were all picked up in a vehicle. All the killings were sexually motivated, although they were not all raped. It really looked to the press, public and some police officers that they had a maniac on the loose.

The police were working on the assumption that Anna Kenny had been taken by a long-distance lorry driver (shades of Agnes Cooney) as they were most likely to carry a shovel in their cab in case they become bogged down in snow on quiet country roads. Detectives visited road-haulage firms and asked them to supply details of all drivers who had made runs to the Campbeltown area in August 1977.

But Anna Kenny's mother believed that her daughter was not likely to take a lift from a lorry driver. She would only have climbed willingly into a taxi. A taxi . . . It was something that came into the hunt again and again. Three of the victims had left places of entertainment to find a taxi.

Detectives were hedging their bets, however. They firmly believed their killer – now officially being named a mass killer – had assaulted other women but had not killed them. They appealed once more to other women who had been assaulted by a man yet had not reported the incident to come forward now. They could hold a vital clue. 'We are anxious for information from any woman who, since the beginning of August 1977, has been given a lift in any vehicle from Glasgow city centre – in particular the Townhead area,' said Detective Superintendent Ian McGill of the Serious Crime Squad, 'and who was subsequently molested by the driver. This also applies to any women who have accepted lifts on the road north, especially to the Argyll area.'

They were certain that the answer to the mystery lay either in Townhead or even in Skipness. The killer had not chosen the area by chance. He may, they reasoned, have had reason to go there, hence the long-distance lorry driver theory. He may also have been a salesman or even a holiday-maker. He could, in fact, have been anyone.

By the beginning of May 1979, the new tourist season was beginning and police leave was cancelled while officers interviewed all travellers who either passed through, stopped or even just lingered in the Skipness area to admire the view. But despite an appeal to three men seen in Lister Street, Glasgow, on the night Anna Kenny disappeared, nothing more of a positive nature was announced.

The killer – or killers – of the four women seemed to have disappeared into thin air. Like Jack the Ripper, like Bible John, the police seemingly never came close to catching him. But then, serial killers are notoriously difficult to catch, at least in this country where police do not have the experience of such madmen as they do in the United States, the acknowledged home of the serial killer.

When they are caught in Britain it is generally by chance. Burke and Hare, who allegedly killed 16 people for the dissection tables of Dr Knox, were apprehended only after they made the mistake of killing a well-known street character. Dennis Nilsen was caught after a man found a suspicious sludge when he was cleaning the drains, while the Yorkshire Ripper was caught by police officers who were suspicious of his behaviour and who had no idea who they had on their hands.

Curiously enough, Peter Sutcliffe, the Yorkshire Ripper, was suspected for a time in the Glasgow murders. Shortly after his conviction in May 1981 for the murder of 13 women, it was revealed that two Lanarkshire women had been conducting affairs with him. They knew him as Peter Logan and met him while he was making regular deliveries to the GM plant at Newhouse. In addition, a woman in Peterhead admitted getting to know him when he made regular trips to oil-based companies in Aberdeen. Sutcliffe drove a lorry similar to the one seen near where Agnes Cooney was thumbing a lift at the Castle Street interchange in Glasgow. Detectives also strongly suspected a lorry driver had taken Anna Kenny to Argyll.

Strathclyde Police sent files on all four Scottish killings to the Ripper Squad in Yorkshire, asking them to check out any possible links. Jim Hobson, then head of the squad, personally checked the files with their own and ruled out any connection. However, in July 1982 two Scottish detectives travelled south to Parkhurst prison on the Isle of Wight to personally interview Sutcliffe. The results of that interview have never been made public and there have been no charges brought. It may be that they did not get much out of the man. Although the jury had decided he was sane and fit to plead, Sutcliffe soon showed strong signs of insanity and within three years of beginning his prison sentence had to be moved from Parkhurst to Broadmoor. It could also be that he had firm alibis for the dates in question.

Another mass killer, who cannot be named for legal reasons, was allegedly implicated in the Hilda McAulay murder by documents found near the body. However, a senior police officer rejected any possibility of a connection by pointing out that his preferred victims were children and he would not have known how to cope with a grown woman. But Hilda McAulay was only five foot tall, while Mary Gallagher was even shorter.

And so the identity of what may be Scotland's forgotten serial killer still remains a mystery. Perhaps the four killings were not in fact connected, unlike the two deaths in the other major murder inquiry of 1977, this time in Edinburgh. In this case, the police obtained a very clear, very precise description of the two prime suspects. But despite that, the men still managed to evade justice. Or did they?

The two girls had known each other most of their lives. They had played together as children, gone to school together, gone on double dates together. In the end, they were both found dead within four miles of each other, strangled, their hands tied tightly behind them.

Christine Eadie and Helen Scott were both 17 years of age. Red-haired Christine was an office worker, blonde Helen a shop assistant in a tartan shop on Edinburgh's Princes Street. On 15 October 1977, they and two female friends walked through the fog-filled streets of the city's famous Royal Mile. It was a Saturday night in a Scottish city and the girls were set to howl. They had been working hard all week, had cash in their purses and did not need to face angry parents when they staggered home in the early hours of the morning: both girls had left home earlier that year. They would go out, have a few drinks – have a lot of drinks – have a few laughs and maybe even get chatted up. Then, maybe, they'd hear about a party and go on somewhere else. What the hell – they were young, free and single. And it was 1977. Everybody was allowed to have a good time in 1977.

The last pub they hit that riotous Saturday night was the World's End bar in the High Street. 'Behind these walls is the World's End' a sign on the wall near the doors said ominously. For Christine and Helen, that sign – which at one time somebody probably thought funny – would be horribly prophetic.

The pub was busy when they arrived, many of the young male customers still loudly discussing the main sporting topic of the week – Scotland's victory over Wales the previous Wednesday night in Liverpool, which set them on the road to the World Cup in Argentina. That Ally's Army would be defeated in South America was not something that could be countenanced, and those who spoke of the prospect spoke with excitement and not a little patriotic fervour. The girls found an empty table near the phone, which Helen used to try and contact her boyfriend, Ian, who was at the time working as a waiter in a Berwickshire hotel. However, she was unable to contact him.

The men hit on the girls soon after they arrived. They were older, late 20s or early 30s, but by that time Christine and Helen had drunk just enough to throw caution to the wind. It was all part of having a good time, right? Anyway, they seemed all right. They were only talking. Both spoke with local accents, both about five foot five inches tall, each of them with short wavy hair. One was stockier than his friend, and wearing pin-striped baggy brown trousers with, distinctively, five buttons at each pocket flap and a high waistband. He was also wearing a brown v-necked jumper and a bright coloured shirt. His friend was of medium build and had a thick dark moustache. He was wearing a blue-grey jumper and black trousers.

The girls' two friends had gone to the toilet and walked back into the smoke and noise of the pub to find the men sitting at their table with Christine and Helen. The men had bought them a drink – whisky and lemonade each – and the four were having a great time, roaring with laughter. When asked if they were coming on to a party, the two girls said no. They were going to stay there. Christine and Helen had, apparently, 'clicked' and the other two friends understood the rules of the game. If Christine and Helen had gone with them to that party, they would still be alive today.

The men and the girls left soon after, the four of them disappearing into the fog-shrouded streets of the old town. What happened between then and the following afternoon is a mystery.

Christine's body was found first, at around two p.m. the following day. A young couple out for a Sunday afternoon stroll on a stretch of foreshore between Aberlady and Longniddry, East Lothian, came across the naked and brutally beaten body lying tucked between sand dunes only 100 yards from the gates leading to the Gosford House estate. Her hands were tied behind her back and she had been strangled with her own tights.

Four hours later, a gardener walking his dog made the second grisly discovery: the semi-naked body of Helen Scott, again savagely beaten and strangled with her hands tied behind her back, this time in a field near the training stables of Lieutenant Commander Wilfred Crawford at Haddington.

The discoveries sparked off what was called one of the biggest manhunts the country had ever seen. The police swiftly set up a mobile headquarters just outside the Gosford House estate, owned by the Earl of Wemyss. Extra police officers were drafted in to assist in the inquiry. Roadblocks were set up on the A198 and every driver stopped and asked where he or she had been on the previous night: had they been on this road? Had they seen anything? Gosford Bay was known as a favourite spot for 'winching' (courting) couples. The police knew it had been especially busy on that Saturday night and they wanted anyone who had used it to talk to them. They may well have seen something. Meanwhile, as fog rolled in from the Firth of Forth, tracker dogs were used to scour the area for further items of clothing and other clues.

The road at the second locus was also sealed off, and as the body was found just as darkness was gathering, forensic scientists studied the ground under the harsh glare of flood-lights powered by generators. Tracker dogs were used to help trace items of clothing still missing. The victims' handbags were never found.

The murdered girls' friends were able to provide detectives with a description of the men in the pub. The comparatively new photofit system was used to build up a picture of the men. (Photofit was first adopted in Britain in 1970, taking the place of the old identikit drawings. There are five groups of facial characteristics – forehead/hair, eyes, nose, mouth, chin/lower jaw – with over 500 different features, which when selected by witnesses can create up to 15 billion facial combinations.)

The faces these and other witnesses selected were copied and issued not just to the 60 officers involved in the actual investigation but also to every policeman and woman in the force. (Within two months the murder team would be reduced to 24 officers. Over the months that followed, it would drop even further.) Detectives travelled round the pubs and clubs in Edinburgh city centre, showing the pictures to customers and staff, the questions always the same – have you seen these men? When did you see them? Who were they with? Did you see them with two girls on Saturday 15 October? Do you know their names, addresses, ages? Anything . . . ?

Their inquiries revealed that the two men had been seen earlier in other pubs on or near the High Street, including the Lorna Doone and the Allan Ramsey. The search for the men widened when the Crown Office gave permission for copies of the photofit of one of the men – the clean-shaven one with the distinctive brown trousers – to be released to newspapers and television stations. Newspapers also printed a photograph of two look-alike policewomen sitting at the same table in the World's End, in the hope that it would attract further witnesses from the bustle of young people who had been in the pub that night. Hopes that the unique design of the suspect's trousers would help pinpoint him were dashed when it was discovered that cut-price tailors were mass-producing them and flooding the street markets of Central Scotland with similar garments.

And despite numerous media appeals, detectives still did not manage to trace everyone who had been in the World's End that night. They also did not have any luck tracing the owners of two suspicious vehicles seen by a number of witnesses in the area of the murders. A dark Ford Transit or Bedford Dormobile was first spotted parked outside the World's End on the Saturday night. Either it or another one similar was seen later that night – at around midnight – three miles from where Helen's body was dumped. A workman told the police that he had seen a man making a telephone call from a public telephone box in the village of Drem. The man was in an extremely agitated state and the dark van had been driven up on to the verge beside the box. It was dark, but the witness, who had been waiting to make a call, said the man had collar-length brown hair and a Mexican-type moustache. The description seemed to tally with that of one of the men in the World's End. However, despite tracking down the owners of 200 such vans, this possible lead took them nowhere.

The other vehicle was a dark, four-door saloon, possibly a Ford Cortina Mark 3. Witnesses had seen such a car parked near Longniddry golf course, not far from Gosford Bay. They said there were three, possibly four, people inside. They said one of them was a blonde girl who looked to be seriously upset. They said she seemed to be trying to get out of the car. They said the car was parked at the east end of the sea-shore carpark, very near a large white van. They said the car drove out of the carpark at high speed.

Later, at about 3.20 a.m. on Sunday morning, a car carrying two men was seen driving swiftly in the direction of the city through Port Seton, less than five miles away from where Christine Eadie's body was found. The occupants of the car spotted in the carpark were never traced. The blonde girl may have been Helen Scott.

As the hunt progressed, the police tried to apply some psychology in an attempt to drive a wedge between the two prime suspects. A doctor who had been following the case informed reporters that if there were indeed two men involved in the murder, then one of them may well have been in danger himself. Both girls had been beaten and strangled with their own tights, then dumped in the remote areas of East Lothian. They had not, however, been sexually assaulted and this suggested that one of the men at least was a sadist and enjoyed inflicting pain. It may even have given him sexual gratification.

This man would have possessed a strong personality, able to dominate not only his victims but perhaps even his accomplice. He may, ultimately, come to realise that his accomplice could implicate him in the murders. And decide that the only way to be certain of that accomplice's continued silence would be to kill him. Dead men, as they say, tell no tales.

The police offered full protection to anyone who came forward with vital information. No one came forward, although two men who answered the descriptions – but were not the men in the pub – approached the police to be cleared of all suspicion.

Someone who certainly did feel at risk was Christine Eadie's friend. The girls' handbags were never found and inside them were address books, almost certainly with her phone number in them. The men may have picked her name up as they talked in the World's End. She had started to receive very strange phone calls. The police never released her name to the press and protected her for as long as was necessary.

Both suspects had short hair, something not uncommon now but certainly unusual in the late seventies. Detectives visited Edinburgh's Redford Barracks and interviewed soldiers of the Queen's Own Highlanders stationed there at the time. They also spoke to members of the Royal Highland Fusiliers at Kirknewton and sailors whose ships were at Rosyth dock-yards.

By early summer of 1978 the hunt was all but over. The police had followed up every lead they could and had still not been able to make an arrest. Then, in June, the hunt dramatically shifted west, when an anonymous letter was received stating that it was two Glasgow men who had killed the girls. The letter said the men had been on holiday in Port Seton, where there were number of holiday chalets and caravans to rent. It was also common for young men to use their parents' caravans for wild weekends of sex and drink. The police interviewed the owners of 700 chalets and caravans in the area. Again, nothing.

There was a suggestion that the men were known criminals and in May 1979 detectives from Edinburgh went to Peterhead prison near Aberdeen after they received a letter from an inmate who claimed another prisoner was the killer. Again, there were no arrests made and no names released.

And just when it seemed the investigation had again run its course, the murders hit the headlines again. In June 1981, almost four years after the killings, the *Daily Record* received yet another anonymous letter saying two men had been overheard talking about the murders, saying they had killed the girls because 'they would not give in to them'. Four days later the newspaper received another letter, posted like the first in the Motherwell and Wishaw area and this time actually naming the two men. Both letters were taken away by detectives for forensic tests. Although they had already received over 30 such letters, all of which had turned out to be disappointments, they were taking these ones seriously. In a murder inquiry like this, the police cannot afford to dismiss anything out of hand and they urged the writer to get in contact with them. If the writer did get in touch, then police never released the fact. The two men named have no doubt been investigated and cleared.

The killers have never been caught. Despite the 15,000 interviews and the 24,000 pages of statements, detectives never seemed to make that one final connection which could put the two men in the dock. The lure of a £1,500 reward, put up by the employers of the two dead girls and that of Helen's father, did not prove tempting enough for the one person with that vital piece of information to come forward. Even another letter, received in the autumn of 1978 and described by police as 'the most promising lead so far', failed to help. The contents of this particular letter have never been revealed but the police did say at the time that the writer did appear to know more about the crimes than had hitherto been released.

The police hate unsolved crimes; mysteries are anathema to them. Perhaps that is why, when there are cases such as these, rumours circulate that they did know who the murderers were but just did not have enough evidence. Such rumours have filtered through in this case, suggesting the killers were two fairly well-known Edinburgh criminals, both now locked up for other serious crimes. The rumours may just be a way for the police to salve their injured pride – names are seldom mentioned in such stories. On the other hand, they could just as easily be true.

But someone out there knows the truth. Killers seldom work in a vacuum. Someone knows – or suspects – what they have done and chooses to ignore it, a wife, perhaps, or a mother or a lover. Someone who should have noticed something out of the ordinary – maybe blood stains, scratches, or even curious mood changes and an abnormal interest in the murder investigation. Someone knew the killer or killers well. Someone cooked their meals and washed their clothes. Someone sat with them, talked with them and slept with them. Someone *knew*. Whoever that someone was, they have kept their secret for over 16 years, through blindness, fear or misplaced loyalty. They have ignored – or been ignorant of – the effects murders such as these have on others. None of these girls had done anything wrong. They had gone out for a night and at some point had met the man, or men, who would somehow charm them, then kill them. The ripples spread out from the act to touch family, friends and even police officers who become involved. Mothers and fathers cannot grieve properly with the knowledge that the person responsible for their child's death is still walking the streets, still going out at weekends, still enjoying themselves while their children lie in their graves.

This applies not only to the deaths of Christine and Helen, but also to the killings of Anna, Hilda, Agnes and Mary in Glasgow. At the time, the police strongly discounted any suggestion of a connection between the Glasgow and Edinburgh cases, even though they themselves investigated the possibility. However, there are disturbing similarities: first and most obviously, the victims were all female; they were all killed at the weekend; they were all picked up at places of entertainment, or were on their way to or from such places; with the exception of Mary Gallagher, they all had hands or ankles bound; again with the exception of Mary, they were all taken in a vehicle and dumped in remote areas; none of them appeared to have been sexually assaulted; and their handbags were missing. And most importantly, the killers appear to have got away with it.

# In a Lonely Place

ON A DARK night in August 1983, a young couple made a trip to the banks of a picturesque loch which boasts some of the most breathtaking views in Central Scotland. But this man and woman were not interested in scenery. They were making the trip at night, walking the 25 miles from Maryhill in the north-west of Glasgow to Balloch on the shores of Loch Lomond, pushing a pram with a three-month-old baby girl inside. There were mysterious forces at work within them, forces which were beyond their control and quite possibly beyond their understanding. Forces which would drive them to infanticide.

Their story is a strange one, mixing murder and madness with the occult and obsessive behaviour. It would be two years before their crime would be discovered and a further six months before they came to trial, a trial which left many questions unanswered.

For although we know who the murderers were, we do not know for sure why they killed, or exactly what happened on that terrible summer night.

Or what happened to the body . . .

It was at the age of ten that Sheena McLaughlan first became fascinated by the occult. That was the day she discovered Dennis Wheatley's black-magic thrillers, and like many another child before and since, she was intrigued by the subject, wanting to learn more. However, unlike other youngsters, Sheena never grew out of it.

She had a love of music and sang in concerts for local under-privileged children. She had ambitions to become a pop singer. She formed two bands but split from them when she decided she was too good for them. She was bright and

73

intelligent, with one psychiatrist later observing that she could talk knowledgeably on a great number of subjects.

But throughout her teenage years her obsession with the occult grew. She became more deeply embroiled in the often murky world, her life being increasingly ruled by tarot cards, which she claimed she used for self-analysis. Later a boyfriend would say that she had a natural ability as well as an acquired skill at reading the cards.

After leaving Woodside secondary school in Glasgow with a clutch of qualifications she entered Edinburgh's Napier College, but her extra-curricular interests had such an effect on her mind that she failed her exams. Finally, in 1982, she travelled to London with a friend to meet an occultist named Dharma. The friend did not linger long in the south but Sheena stayed for some months, eventually returning to her mother's home in the Maryhill area of Glasgow in December 1982. She was 21 years of age. And she was pregnant.

The identity of the father remained a mystery, a mystery that Sheena's mother Flora never solved. She was told that he was a divorced man in London, but Sheena would not divulge his name. But at the same time, Sheena was telling an old school friend that her pregnancy was the result of an immaculate conception which occurred as she walked across Salisbury Plain – thanks to Stonehenge, a site of great significance to New Age followers like Sheena.

Finally though, on 9 May 1983, the child was born. Sheena chose to name the baby girl Kether Boleskin. The first part of the name was the title of the principal Sephiroth – or emanation from God – of the Hebrew tree of life; the second was the name of a house and estate on the shores of Loch Ness once owned by arch-magician Aleister Crowley, the self-styled Great Beast who did much to promote the interest in black magic – or magick as he preferred to term it – earlier this century. But although Sheena cared for her daughter well enough, all was not well.

At the trial almost three years later, witnesses would tell the court of Sheena's spirit guide, a Tibetan monk, who, the girl claimed, appeared to her in saffron robes, and who gave her the chilling warning: 'Your baby has to die.' In her police statement, Sheena herself said: 'I kept getting these premonitions. I kept seeing my baby's head covered in blood. I thought she was going to die. I heard voices in my mind.'

At this time, Sheena felt the only person she could turn to was Alan Porter, a painter and decorator who claimed to be a spiritual healer. The pair had met in the spring of 1983. She confided in him – and her father Henry who was divorced from her mother but lived nearby. She said she felt that Flora, her mother, was going to take the baby away from her. In the summer of 1983, grandmother Flora went on holiday to Florida. She would never see little Kether again.

On 26 August Sheena and Alan made their trip to the shores of Loch Lomond. There, on that hill overlooking a little beach, with the cold waters of the loch whispering softly on the shingle and the wind sighing through the trees, they murdered little Kether. In the two years that followed they were both haunted by their act. Only they knew what had happened to little Kether and what they had done on that fateful August night. Now, over ten years later, that is still the case.

On the phone to her mother, Sheena said that the baby was fine and was being well taken care of. Later, she claimed that Kether had gone to live with her father in England. But by the time Flora returned from holiday, her daughter was gone. She and Porter left Scotland, travelling to Brighton to stay with friends of his. Sheena did not take to life in England and the enormity of what they had done preyed on her mind. One night, after she had been 'awful upset' (her words), they left Brighton and returned north, staying with other friends on a croft in North Uist. But these friends found McLaughlan somewhat too intense for their tastes and they asked her to leave. Soon after they returned to Porter's home in Glasgow's Gorbals, the couple split up.

Sheena went to live with William Borland, whom she had met through Porter. They lived in a caravan at Errogie in Inverness-shire – ironically, only a few miles from Foyers and Boleskin House. During the time they lived together, Sheena broke her silence and for the first time she spoke of the night her child died, claiming that Alan Porter had murdered Kether. 'Alan's eyes were bulging and his face was red,' she had told her new boyfriend. 'It was like a great ritual.'

In May 1984, he and Sheena made an emotional journey back to the scene of the murder, back to that small hill overlooking the shingle beach. Here Sheena left Borland for an hour to find the child's makeshift grave. But all she found was the baby's bottle and a hairbrush. The body would never be found. Sheena was in a highly distressed state, wailing and screaming as she claimed Porter had killed the child, saying that her baby's spirit was all around her.

Eventually, Borland's relationship with this unbalanced girl came to an end and in August 1985, Sheena phoned her mother in Glasgow, telling her she was in Scotland and that she planned to revive her singing ambitions by making a pop record. When asked of the baby, Sheena told her mother that little Kether had died of cancer. Sheena also claimed to have cancer herself. One week later, when Sheena had returned to Glasgow, the truth came out during a conversation with her mother and father. Kether was dead and buried at Loch Lomond – and Porter had murdered her.

The shocked grandmother contacted Maryhill police office who then referred the case to Dumbarton police, where it became the responsibility of the head of CID, Detective Chief Inspector Adam Hay. A veteran of 31 years on the Force, DCI Hay, now retired, had worked on a great many murder cases – including acting as collator during the hunt for Bible John. In his ten years as head of Dumbarton's detective squad he investigated a total of 23 murders. But none like this. 'It was one of the strangest investigations I've ever worked on,' he said. 'A baby death is always distressing but this one was more than that – it was bizarre . . .'

However, before he could properly interview Sheena McLaughlan, the woman suffered a nervous breakdown and was being treated in Stobhill hospital's psychiatric unit. Her doctor suggested that they leave her alone for a week or two. That suited the police. It gave them time to contact every agency they could think of to try and trace the child, including adoption agencies and the Salvation Army. 'I worked with three officers from the female and child unit and they really pulled out all the stops,' said Adam Hay. 'If that child was alive they were determined to find her. But no one knew anything about her.' Of course not, because what Sheena McLaughlan said was the truth – Kether had been strangled and her body left beside the loch.

According to Sheena, Porter had given her some sort of drug on that frightful night in August 1983 and made her walk to the lochside, pushing the baby's pram before her. She said he had wanted her to make some sort of decision regarding the baby because they wanted to go away and Kether was apparently a hindrance to their plans. 'The baby was crying,' she told police. 'I gave her a bottle but she kept on crying. Alan was angry because the baby was crying and wouldn't stop.' Finally, Porter took the child from her and she went for a walk and when she returned he told her that Kether was dead. Then they returned to Glasgow but she did not remember how. Porter, though, would later tell a slightly different version.

But before then, Sheena was to make one more journey back to the lochside, this time in the company of the police. They had been searching at the water's edge because her original statement had suggested that was where the murder took place. But she took them to a spot high on a hill, overlooking the loch. She pointed to the small burn where she had washed the child's face, fed her and changed her nappy. And she pointed out the spot where she claimed Porter had taken the baby from her. And while she walked through the dense woods, all the memories must have come flooding back to her because she broke down into hysterical sobbing and had to be comforted by a policewoman and an old friend who had agreed to come with her.

Sheena McLaughlan was allowed to go home while they continued their search. They found items of the baby's clothing and a bottle but no body. 'The body could have been carried off by foxes or badgers,' observed Adam Hay, 'or even washed away in heavy storms and floods. There was just no trace of it.' Park rangers interviewed by officers recalled finding a pram in good condition near the spot, which they handed in to Alexandria police station some time before. Records were checked and they discovered that the pram was eventually passed on to McAteer's Salerooms, who dispose of unclaimed property held by Strathclyde Police. However, the ultimate owner was never found.

Meanwhile, DCI Hay and his team had managed to track down Alan Porter. It was not easy because Porter was not, as they say, known to the police. Eventually, though, they found his mother's address in the Anderston area of Glasgow. Mrs Porter proved to be most helpful, explaining that her son had 'turned funny' and had left the house. However, she hadn't a clue where he was at that time. Through the DHSS, Adam Hay found an address for Porter in Aberdeen but a quick check by local officers showed that he had moved on – to Hove in Sussex. Another call was made to local officers, asking them to detain the man for questioning regarding a child murder. The English officers moved swiftly. Within an hour, Adam Hay took a telephone call from his opposite number in Hove telling him that they had Porter in custody. DCI Hay and WPC Doreen Baines of the female and child unit travelled overnight to interview the man the policeman would later describe as 'the strangest fellow I have ever met'.

On 27 September, 1985, in a small interview room in Hove police station, Porter willingly – almost gratefully – rhymed off his version of the murder. He confirmed that he and Sheena had wheeled the baby's pram from Glasgow to Stablewood in Balloch country park – but there his story differed subtly but importantly from the one already given by the girl. He said that he saw Sheena trying to choke the child first by putting her fingers down her throat. 'I saw that the baby was suffering so I put it out of its suffering,' he told the police officers. 'I was crying. I was exploding. The sweat was running down my face. I lost my initial stability and I strangled it with my bare hands. I took it away and laid it down. It was dead, it seemed dead. I laid it down in the wood beside a small burn. It was wrapped in a small blanket. I think it was pink coloured. It was a heartbreaking thing to do.'

He continued: 'I can take you to the spot. I loved that child. I was a fool to follow her. She used me to do it. I cannot live with my conscience'. He also claimed that after he had killed the baby, McLaughlan had wanted to have sex with him in the woods. But he had refused. 'That was the furthest thing from my mind,' he stated.

So, there were two conflicting stories. Sheena said that Porter wanted to get rid of the child, took her away and killed her. Porter claimed that Sheena was the one who wanted Kether to die and had actually set the murderous process in motion.

The trial began in January 1986. Despite their confessions to the police, both accused denied murdering the baby. Sheena McLaughlan lodged a special plea that she was insane at the time and blamed Porter. In turn, Porter claimed that he was under McLaughlan's control mentally at the time and that there was nothing he could do but follow her commands. His counsel was pleading a defence of *folie à deux*, a rare mental disorder in which a receptive person can be cross-infected by a dominant partner suffering from a mental illness such as schizophrenia. It is not an easy defence to make, but Porter's lawyers made a brave stab at it.

Meanwhile, psychiatrists, in deciding that the pair were sane and fit to plead, had already stated that they could not express an opinion about their mental state at the time of the murder, two-and-a-half years before. McLaughlan was certainly obsessed with herself. While she was a voluntary patient in Stobhill hospital, she had told a doctor that she was 'too intellectual' for others and that she saw things in the clouds. She had described herself as a scientific person who used the tarot to analyse herself and that she possessed great insight. Alan Porter, meanwhile, had told another psychiatrist that he had been under her control and that she possessed 'a great spiritual force'. He claimed that she told him: 'The baby has to die.'

The doctor had first examined Porter while he was in

Barlinnie Prison in October 1985 and at first the man had refused to discuss what had happened on the lochside two years before. However, the doctor visited the accused again and he did give him an account, again slightly different from what he said originally but still at odds with Sheena McLaughlan's recollection. He said that they had been arguing about the baby. 'Sheena said the baby had to die,' he told the doctor. 'Sheena was holding the baby with her hand round its neck. I don't know what she was trying to do.' He went on to say that he wrapped the baby's body in the blanket and placed it in a small burn with only a trickle of water. All the time, Sheena was with him, he said. 'I don't know if it was alive or dead.' Then they walked from the loch to Drymen. 'Sheena was very powerful spiritually at the time. She was like an angel and had control of the situation.' He claimed that he had been under her control since leaving the house in Glasgow and said she had a great spiritual force guiding her all the way. He had no idea if he could have resisted that force.

Events in Drymen go some way to underline Porter's claim. After the murder, Sheena walked into the local police station, claiming that her bag had been stolen and they had no money to get back to Glasgow. She asked the police officer for a lift back to Milngavie. The officer observed that the girl seemed confident while Porter sat outside on a wall, waiting. The question remains if this was the action of a woman who was under the control of a dominant male.

Neither accused gave evidence during the nine-day trial although their police statements were read out to the jury. During WPC Baines's testimony regarding Porter's interview in Hove police station, McLaughlan broke down in the dock, sobbing loudly. The trial judge, Lord Wylie, halted the proceedings and the woman was led from the dock. The following day, her face deathly pale, she changed her plea to guilty on a reduced charge of culpable homicide. The plea was accepted and she was taken from the court to await sentencing after the trial.

This left Porter alone on the charge of murder. Throughout the trial he had listened impassively to the evidence against him. His hair long and his face bearded, his skin pale, his eyes dark and piercing, he looked just the way a murderous black magician would be expected to look. But on the second last day of the trial, while he listened to his counsel call for leniency as he detailed the effects McLaughlan's madness had on him, he bowed his head and wept silently.

The jury took just over an hour to find him guilty of murder and he was sentenced to life. It was only the third time in Scottish legal history that an accused had been found guilty of murder without a body. The first was in 1962 in Glasgow when a four-year-old child was murdered and the other in 1980 involving the death of a 57-year-old man in Lanarkshire.

The famous *corpus delecti* beloved of crime fiction is not, as many believe, the actual corpse of the victim. The term relates to the essentials of the murder and the circumstances relating to it. In a murder case, the prosecution need only prove that the death has in fact occurred and that the killing was unlawful – no actual body is required. Perhaps the most famous British case is the kidnapping and murder of Mrs Muriel McKay in 1968 by the Husein brothers. It is believed that her body was fed to the pigs in Rook's farm, Hertfordshire. Since the Kether Boleskin case, three men were convicted in 1989 of the murder of a drug courier on Fenwick Moor. The victim's body was never discovered – and indeed, one of the convicted men has claimed that he is not even dead.

On 13 February 1986, Sheena McLaughlan was sentenced to five years for her part in the death. The Crown accepted she had been suffering from diminished responsibility. Kevin Drummond, prosecuting, had told Lord Wylie that there was no question of mental disorder, mental handicap or mental illness. However, medical reports did reveal that although hospital treatment was not necessary, the accused might benefit from psychiatric help. Donald Robertson QC, defending, pointed out there was no evidence that she had assaulted the child but what she had done was acquiesce in handing the child over to Porter. Lord Wylie, though, said she must have realised Porter would do something to the baby. She had, in fact, abandoned responsibility for the child. 'This young woman doesn't appear even now to have any remorse. In the latest medical reports it would appear her mind is still deranged and she is still involved in the spirit world.' He described the crime as violent and said that the five-year sentence would reflect the repugnance of society. But there are those – police officers, journalists, lawyers – who believe that McLaughlan got off lightly and should have received an identical sentence to Porter.

As to what really happened that night, we will probably never know. All that is certain is that the child died but as to who began the killing process and what subsequently occurred, we only have the differing descriptions of the two accused. As for what happened to the body, perhaps Adam Hay's assumptions are correct. Perhaps the dead baby was carried off by animals or washed away by heavy rains. After all, there is not much to a three-month child and two years of Scottish weather would have taken their toll.

# The Whistleblower

*It may have happened like this . . .*

HE HAD BEEN travelling for about four hours before he knew they were there. But by that time it was too late.

He could not have been totally sure who they were because all he could see was a pair of headlights burning in his rear-view mirror – but he could make an educated guess. He pressed his foot down on the accelerator, just to see if they too picked up speed. It was pitch dark now but he was not concerned about that. He had driven this road many times over the past 20 years and knew every curve, every dip, every sudden turn. Flicking his eyes from the road ahead, where the twin shafts of his own headlights picked out the luminous road markings at the side of the narrow road, and back to his rear view, he saw that the car behind was keeping pace with him.

Then there was a second set of beams, piercing the darkness ahead of him, rising and falling with each slough in the road, speeding towards him straight down the middle, not stopping, not slowing, not veering to the side but heading right at him. At the last minute he spun the wheel to the left and his car flew off the tarmac and careered down the sharp hillside, bouncing over the grass and bracken, recoiling off rocks, and coming to rest sharply in a stream which erupted from a concrete culvert beneath the road. The two cars stopped in a lay-by on the road above and the men who climbed out, merely shadows in the dark of the Highland night, began to follow the car's path down the hillside.

But he did not know anything of this. He lay slumped in his seat, unconscious. He was not aware of the grim-faced men as they looked through the car window at him, did not see the gun being aimed at him or hear the loud explosion as the trigger was pulled or even feel the bullet as it entered his brain . . .

The man and his wife were heading north on holiday when they found it. They were driving along the A87 from Invergarry, a beautiful run through some stunning scenery towards the Kyle of Lochalsh where the ferries await to take travellers over the short stretch of sea to the splendours of Skye.

It was about ten a.m. on Saturday, 6 April 1985, and the Australian holidaymakers were on a stretch of the road over-looking Loch Loyne. They were talking, occasionally glancing at the scenery as it sped past. But it was a dull day with the threat of rain, the weather closing in on the hills and the heather. The route is one of the most beautiful in Scotland, affording breathtaking vistas above Loch Garry and on through Glen Shiel towards the castle at Eilean Donan, jutting proudly and highly photogenically into Loch Duich. Compared to those stretches, the view along Loch Loyne is not that breathtaking, although it has its own rough-hewn charm. Bleak, and in 1986 treeless, the only features of note apart from the far-off mountains are the dam which created the loch and the grey granite rocks looming sharply on the far side.

Then the couple caught a glimpse of a splash of deep red, about 100 yards below the road on the hillside. They were past it before it registered: a car, apparently lying abandoned. By the time they had decided to turn back to investigate they had driven another three miles. The man turned his car and sped back in the direction they had come, parking his own vehicle in the small lay-by before he and his wife scrambled down the moist grass to the seemingly crashed car.

It was a maroon Volvo 244, lying at a sharp angle facing south in what appeared to be a small burn, the driver's door wedged solidly against the bank. As they approached they saw that the rear window was shattered. The driver's window was wound fully down and through it they could see the man slumped in the seat, his hands folded on his lap, the car keys lying beside them. His head hung limply against his right shoulder, blood oozing copiously from his temple.

Obviously there had been an accident, the car probably travelling too fast on the narrow road, going out of control as it rounded a sharp bend before leaving the road, tumbling down the hillside. But there was no sign of any major damage, apart from a dent on the roof and the smashed rear window. Even the windscreen was still in place: at least according to this witness – another who arrived later said it was also shattered. However, everyone agreed there was no glass on the inside of the vehicle.

The man ran back up the hillside to the road and flagged down a car he could see coming from the Invergarry direction. He explained to the occupants – Mr David Coutts, his wife, Alison, Dr Dorothy Messer and her fiancé, George Lochhead – that there had been an accident, pointing to the car below them. Other cars began to arrive, slowing – as drivers do – to see what all the fuss was about. One driver agreed to speed on to the nearest phone and alert the emergency services.

Back at the maroon Volvo, as the soft Highland rain began to gently caress the hillside, Mr Coutts was surprised to see that the injured man was someone he knew. Mr Coutts was an SNP councillor in Dundee and he recognised the man as William McRae, a leading figure in the party. Doctor Messer took the injured man's pulse and announced that he was still alive. However, she saw that one pupil was extremely dilated, a strong sign of extensive brain damage. And so they all waited for the ambulance to arrive.

They did not know it, but they were present at the birth of a mystery which has puzzled friends of William McRae for nine years. For it became clear some time after he was discovered on that rain-swept hillside that the man had not been injured in a car crash but had been shot. The authorities insist he died by his own hand. His friends and other investigators claim there is a much more sinister explanation.

William McRae was an eminent man. He was born in 1923 in the small village of Carron, near Falkirk. As a youngster he was incredibly bright, showing enviable debating skills while attending Falkirk high school. He also joined the Scottish National Party during his time at school. Eventually, he became vice-chairman of the Party, standing in a number of elections and coming close to wresting the Ross and Cromarty seat from the Conservatives in 1974. Later, though, he grew dissatisfied with the way the Party was progressing, seeing some of the leadership as 'shallow'. But all that came later in his eventful life.

He studied history at Glasgow University, graduating with first-class honours. He also edited a local newspaper in Grangemouth before entering the services as a lieutenant in the Seaforth Highlanders. It was during a posting to India – then still part of that lumbering giant called the British Empire – that he transferred to the Royal Indian Navy, becoming the youngest captain in the service, taking command of a destroyer and learning to speak both Urdu and Hindi fluently.

His attachment to the country and its culture did not stop there, however. A staunch Scottish nationalist, he became a committed Indian nationalist also. One of his naval duties was to recruit Indians to the service. However, many of them were unwilling to join what was seen as the British Navy. McRae apparently pointed out to them they would need a navy when they gained independence and this was an ideal way to take control, so they signed on the dotted line. They trusted him, because William McRae was an eminent man.

According to some accounts he joined the Indian Congress Party – although after his death his brother denied this. However, even having sympathy for the Indian nationalist cause could have been seen by some as treasonable. He was, after all, an officer in the King's Service, being promoted to lieutenant-commander and then full commander. As the war ended, he transferred to Naval Intelligence, remaining in India, allegedly helping in the running of an illegal radio station espousing the nationalist cause. If caught, this would have left him open to all sorts of charges. He might even have been shot as a traitor.

When he left the service and returned to Scotland, McRae went back to university to take an LLB. As usual, he proved extremely able and outspoken, being declared the most outstanding law student of his year and winning a number of prizes. When he joined the law firm of Abraham Levy in Glasgow, his grasp of Asian languages and culture proved useful in handling the affairs of clients from the city's burgeoning Indian and Pakistani population. He also lectured in law at the University of Glasgow for a period, the halls of academe recognising that he was an eminent man.

His nationalist beliefs grew with his reputation. He was even said to be involved in the hiding of the Stone of Destiny, stolen – or liberated, depending on your point of view – from the Houses of Parliament by a group of daring young Scots students on Christmas Eve, 1950. His support for nationalist causes abroad continued, striking up personal friendships with leaders such as David Ben Gurion, who was in the forefront of the often violent attempts to establish the Palestinian homeland for Jews after the war, resulting in Israel being recognised by the United Nations in May 1948. McRae helped the fledgling state frame its mercantile laws, allegedly lecturing for a time in Haifa – again denied by his brother. However, it seems a plaque to his memory was erected in 1986 at Migdal Ha'Emek in Gallilee which reads: 'In loving memory of a Scottish patriot and faithful friend of Israel.' And as his legal career flourished, he was able to buy a holiday cottage in his beloved Highlands, at Camuslongart in Dornie, Wester Ross.

McRae was an outspoken man, not afraid to speak his mind or to oppose injustice when he saw it. Some would say he was aggressive. His bluntness of speech often offended, for he could lack tact, but he spoke the truth as he saw it. As longstanding friend Michael Strathern put it: 'Three words sum up Willie – truth, integrity and compassion.' His old friend continued: 'He had a tremendously magnetic personality, charisma I suppose you would call it. He would get up and lead and the people would follow. That was the sort of man he was. And that's what made him dangerous to some people.'

He had no fear of authority, perhaps spurred by his nationalist beliefs. In fact, he had the laudable tendency to take on the establishment at every given opportunity. In 1972 he helped fishermen fight Ministry of Defence plans to establish a torpedo testing range in the Inner Sound of Raasay. It was the beginning of an anti-establishment struggle which would not endear him to the faceless men who forever lurk in the secret corridors of power.

A passionate anti-nuclear campaigner, perhaps his greatest triumph came in 1980 when he helped skewer the Atomic Energy Commission over their plans to dump nuclear waste in a site of great beauty in Ayrshire. The public inquiry – known as the Mullwharcher Inquiry – was set to begin in Ayr town hall on 19 February 1980 and run for a few days. Willie McRae, representing the SNP on the list of protesters, and members of various heavyweight environmental groups, questioned the commission's representatives for four weeks, finally winning a ban on the proposal. There were those who said their victory sounded the death knell for such plans in Scotland. It was largely due to that most eminent man, William McRae. After his death, further plans were announced to dump deadly nuclear waste in Scotland's most beautiful countryside.

His exploits in and out of various inquiry rooms would without a doubt have brought McRae to the attention of the security services. His nationalistic beliefs and his desire to blow the whistle on whatever skulduggery the authorities got up to in Scotland were more than enough to have his name placed on the 'subversive list'. Eminent he may have been, but he was also a thorn in their side.

In the same year as the Mullwharcher inquiry, word reached nationalists that secret tests for possible nuclear-waste dumping were to take place in Glen Etive, north-east of Oban. Michael Strathern was one of the activists who formed the Oystercatcher group – named after Ben Trilleachan, the gaelic word for oystercatcher and the area where the tests were to be made. Using simple logic, they reasoned that as no nuclear dumping was to be allowed, thanks to the Mullwharcher Inquiry, then there was really no point in making test bores. A caravan was set up in Glen Etive which was to be manned 24 hours a day, seven days a week by young members of *Siol Nan Gaidtheal* (seed of the gael), an SNP splinter group which believed that actions spoke louder than words. Willie McRae was also a member of this group, having been attracted to it by its direct approach to nationalist matters as well as its youthful exuberance. He wholly approved of the Oystercatcher project. 'Some of the boys were a bit rough,' conceded Michael Strathern, who was in his late 50s at the time. 'Most of them had never seen a wage packet and were more acquainted with a giro cheque. But they had a degree of guts and spunk which was missing from the Scottish Nationalist Party.'

The idea behind the Oystercatcher operation was to prevent the scientists from making their tests. The geologists were said to be working in the area undercover so as not to excite any undue attention. But attention was duly excited. Geologists were caught trying to get into the area posing as hill walkers. They were sent away and told in no uncertain terms never to return again. Researchers from an Edinburgh-based geological institute were also stopped, and a member of the Oystercatchers managed to read documents which were sitting on the front seat of their Land Rover. One of the documents warned geologists not to go out singly to the test area as there were 'harmful elements' in the vicinity. 'This pleased us enormously,' said Michael Strathern. Eventually, Willie McRae borrowed a plane and flew the length of Glen Etive, looking for signs of test drilling. He could see none. The Oystercatcher operation had succeeded.

The caravan at the foot of Ben Trilleachan became the rallying point for many Scots who had embraced the nationalist cause, whether it was for political, personal or more sinister reasons. Among them was a man called David Dinsmore, who would later become the national organiser for *Siol Nan*

*Gaidtheal.* According to some reports, it was McRae's friendship with this man which may have led to his death.

During the two-year Glen Etive campaign, reports began to reach newspapers that young men were receiving military training in the area. One, dressed in paramilitary gear, was photographed burning the Union Jack. He told a reporter from the *Lochaber Free Press:* 'Nuclear waste will not be dumped in Glen Etive or in any part of this land – only over the geologists' dead bodies. Any landowner who allows drilling to take place will be dealt with.' Thankfully, no geologist was asked to lay down his life for his profession and most of the local landowners were against the tests anyway. But it did show an alarming trend towards violence among some of the fringe groups which clung to the nationalist banner.

There is, however, no evidence that Willie McRae supported violent means to political ends. When *Siol Nan Gaidtheal* was formed in the late seventies, they liked to sport ceremonial daggers – the *sgian dhu* – at demonstrations and marches. These long, lethal-looking weapons were worn in direct contravention of the law. It was Willie McRae who finally convinced them it was not necessary to wear them in public.

Eventually though, he felt it necessary to resign from *Siol Nan Gaidtheal.* As he explained on the phone one day to Michael Strathern, some of their activities – which were more of nuisance value than overtly dangerous to the well-being of the nation – had become embarrassing. For instance, demonstrations would often end in a local pub and as the intake of alcohol grew, so did the likelihood of violence. Willie McRae liked a drop of the water of life as much as the next person – some would say somewhat more than the next person – but as a well-respected solicitor, he felt he could not be associated with them any more.

His motives for leaving the group fly in the face of those rumour-mongers who, for whatever reasons, circulated stories of his involvement in so-called tartan terrorism. His supporters point out that if he could not be associated with a group which was doing silly things like removing a gold lectern from St Albans, stolen centuries ago from Holyrood Abbey by marauding English troops, then it is unlikely that he would run the risk of having anything to do with potentially lethal acts like letter bombs and fire attacks. (Incidentally, at the time of writing, that gold lectern is still being hidden somewhere in Scotland.)

However, he was linked speculatively to a cheeky but potentially dangerous operation in 1981 designed to draw attention to one of the forgotten atrocities of the Second World War. In their desire to defeat Hitler and the Nazis, the British government engaged in some shameful biological warfare experimentation, resulting in the development at the government laboratories in Porton Down, Wiltshire, of anthrax spores which the War Office, with Churchill's blessing, planned to drop over German cities, including Berlin. Naturally, the device used to trigger this lethal germ had to be tested and the tiny island of Gruinard, off the west coast of Scotland, was chosen as a site.

The plan to attack the Third Reich with germs was never carried out but unfortunately the tests left this small Scottish island uninhabitable to either man or beast. Although rare among humans, anthrax is highly infectious – and lethal – in cattle and sheep. When contracted by humans, usually those who handle animals' hides or bone-meal, it can cause boils on the skin, serious breathing difficulties and gastro-intestinal problems. Generally though, it can be treated successfully with penicillin. But the spores can lie dormant in the soil for an unlimited amount of time – unless treated. Signs were posted on the mainland near the island as well as Gruinard's shore warning any unwary sailor or swimmer that they could not land.

The shameful episode was forgotten by most Scots until October 1981, when Scottish newspapers received letters from the grandly named Dark Harvest Commando of the Scottish Citizen Army. They said that they were a group of microbiologists from two Scottish universities and claimed to have landed on Gruinard and taken about 300 lbs of infected soil. They said a portion of the soil, what they called 'the seeds of death', had been sent to Porton Down, the birthplace of the original anthrax spores. Searchers found a plastic bucket containing a small portion of earth at the laboratories, which when analysed turned out to be infected with anthrax.

The police moved quickly to try and track down the persons responsible, taking a copy of the letter from the offices of the *Scotsman* for examination and analysis. They also found a diver's mask on the beach near to Gruinard. But they never traced the thieves, leaving the raid one of the many mysteries attached to tartan terrorism.

Meanwhile, politicians and environmental groups condemned the theft as 'totally irresponsible'. The thieves had claimed they had taken every safety precaution but it still did not satisfy everybody. The Ministry of Defence said that they put staff through seven months of immunisation processes before being allowed to set foot on the island, while Mr Hamish Grey, MP for Ross and Cromarty and an energy minister, said: 'These people have put the whole country in danger. It was like somebody going to an area affected by rabies, taking a few animals home with them and then distributing them around the countryside,' he thundered. However, he also said if it was a hoax, he would see it as a perfectly legitimate way of focusing attention on the problem.

On 14 October, 1981, another soil sample was found by a workman in a locked lift-wheel office 390 feet up Blackpool Tower. It looked as if the small plastic container had been pushed under the door. The town was at that time playing host to the annual Conservative Party conference. This sample, too, was analysed and said to be from Gruinard but was not infected with the deadly anthrax spore. It seems that by this time the island had only certain so-called 'hot spots' – sections of land which were still infected. This sample had obviously been taken from a non-infected part of the island.

After that, there was no further word from Dark Harvest Commando, although there was a hoax claim that the ground at Hampden Park stadium had been covered with the remaining soil. However, public opinion had been stimulated by the operation and eventually the government announced a plan to treat the remaining hot spots with detergent and water in a bid to 'defuse' the biological time-bomb. Dark Harvest had succeeded in its aims.

Although McRae's name has been linked to the operation, there is again no evidence of any direct connection. But given his nationalist connections, it was always possible that he knew who the Dark Harvest Commando were and possibly even approved of their actions.

Some of those connections were, allegedly, part of the Scottish National Liberation Army (SNLA), a group responsible for a number of letter-bomb attacks between March 1982 and December 1983 on, among others, Margaret Thatcher, Norman Tebbit, Michael Heseltine, Malcolm Rifkind and even the Queen herself. A small device sent to Downing Street in November 1982 exploded causing only minor damage. Another, larger device, went off in Woolwich Arsenal in 1983. There was an explosion in the office of Glasgow Lord Provost Michael Kelly on the day of a visit to the city by Princess Diana in 1983. And in 1985, a blaze in the basement of the MOD headquarters in Whitehall caused thousands of pounds worth of damage. All the work of the SNLA. Members claimed there were other attacks which were hushed up by the authorities.

According to a July 1989 report in *Observer Scotland*, a spokesman for the SNLA claimed that two bombs had been placed some years before on approach roads to Coulport nuclear base, causing the base to be sealed off for a full day. He also alleged that Willie McRae had been involved in the planning of the attack. But no direct evidence has ever been produced linking the man with terrorist acts.

There were reports that Willie McRae not only knew members of the SNLA but was in fact deeply involved as the organisation's paymaster. Special Branch surveillance on him was said to have been stepped up and he even allegedly told a friend that his 'cover had been blown', although this could have been a tongue-in-cheek comment. McRae knew some of his 'shadows' by sight as they turned up on a number of occasions at public meetings where he was speaking. The allegations of direct involvement in terrorism (little more than rumours as no evidence has ever been released to back them up) infuriated both his family and friends when they began to circulate following his death. They insist that Willie McRae would not have had anything to do with violent acts.

One of the men allegedly at the heart of many of these attacks was David Dinsmore. The other was Adam Busby. Both are in self-imposed exile, having fled the country in 1984 with bombing and conspiracy charges over their heads. McRae had links with both of them. He may even have had firm knowledge of their whereabouts in 1985. That knowledge, according to some speculation, may have cost him his life. And, although he was an eminent man, his death has never been fully explained.

Willie McRae had already escaped death once that Easter weekend in 1985. He was a committed smoker, like many others with the unfortunate tendency to light up while in bed. On Thursday night, after he returned to his home in Glasgow's Queen's Park at the end of an evening at a friend's house, he fell asleep while smoking. The cigarette naturally dropped on to the bed and in the early hours of the morning he was awakened by the fumes from the smouldering blankets. He leaped out of bed, grabbed the bedclothes and ran into the bathroom with them. Dropping them in the sink, he turned on the tap. However, he had just had a new acrylic bathroom suite fitted and it, too, burst into flames. Soon the flat was filled with thick dark smoke, spotted by two workmen passing in the street as it belched out of a window. One of the men ran to phone the fire brigade while the other forced his way into the flat to find Willie McRae lying in the hallway, overcome by fumes. While fireman put out the blaze in the bathroom, McRae was taken to a neighbouring flat. Covered in soot and embarrassed by what had happened, he refused to see a doctor. When told his bathroom suite was a write-off he said: 'I never did like it.'

He was due to leave that evening to spend the weekend at

his holiday cottage. He was, it seems, writing a book about the nuclear industry, which he had opposed for so many years, and had confided to friends that he had found out something important. However, whether that 'something important' concerned his nuclear researches or another matter has never been made clear. His neighbours saw him leave at about half past six on the evening of Friday, 5 April 1985. He had with him his briefcase containing files, important papers and his notes for the book. Neither the briefcase nor the notes were seen again.

His normal route took him along the western shore of Loch Lomond, through Glencoe, past Fort William, Spean Bridge and on to Invergarry where he would turn on to the A87 to Dornie, about three-quarters of the way along the road to Kyle of Lochalsh. If traffic was with him, he could make the trip in about four hours. It seems that at about half past nine he had to stop outside Invergarry to change a flat tyre, replacing it with a brand new one and placing the punctured one in the rear seat of his car, not in the boot. Then he continued his journey towards Dornie.

According to the official explanation, he was travelling too fast on the narrow road, had been drinking and his car left the road at Loch Loyne. Here, he was so overcome with remorse that he took out his gun – which he had taken to carrying with him at all times – test fired it once and then placed it against his head and pulled the trigger a second time. The bullet lodged in his brain.

But what caused that remorse? Rumours began to circulate shortly after his death. Many of them are red herrings. In fact, this case has more red herrings than a pre-Glasnost Soviet trawler. For instance, one of the strongest rumours was that Willie McRae was homosexual. According to friends and relatives alike, this allegation is wholly without foundation. But the story has gathered in strength until even people who have never met the man repeat it as fact, infuriating those who did know him. But even if he was homosexual why should that force him to kill himself? This was 1985, not 1885, and homosexuality was, in general, accepted. Unless of course he feared what such a revelation, if made in the press, would do to his professional and political standing. There are still people who believe that if you are gay, you must also be perverted and liable to molest children.

Another reason for his supposed suicide was that he was having business problems. Certainly, he had left Levy McRae and set up in a new practice in 1981, but no evidence of any major problems has come to light.

Then it was said that his involvement with the SNLA and hints of connections to other tartan terrorist groups had been discovered. He did tell some friends shortly before his death that he was under surveillance. But then he was a so-called 'subversive' – as anyone who opposes the will of government is seen as a 'subversive' – so he would be under some form of surveillance.

They said he was suffering from some vague unspecified illness. They said he was mentally unsound and had been consulting a psychiatrist for years, who supposedly told him his alcoholism had been caused by his inability to come to terms with his homosexuality.

They said he killed himself to prevent his family suffering the humiliation of a drink-driving offence. He had already been convicted of one such offence and had a second hanging over him. If he had been drinking the night he died – although according to one account it would appear there was no alcohol found in his bloodstream – then that would have been a third.

They said he had been discussing suicide for some time, that he had planned to kill himself on this weekend. Yet he had made appointments to see clients the following week. He had bumped into one of them the day before he left for the Highlands as he came out of a Glasgow bookshop, his arms full of new books he planned to read.

Not only that, but he had placed his name on the list of objectors at the proposed Dounreay Inquiry, which ironically began exactly one year after his death. Can these be seen as the actions of a man planning his own death?

Rumours and conjecture. Theories and ideas. The author-

*Moira Anderson, the Coatbridge girl who disappeared into the snow in 1957*

*Rene Macrae and her three-year-old son, Andrew, who vanished in 1976, leaving behind a burnt-out BMW (Picture courtesy of the Scottish* Sun)

*Detectives examining all that was left of Mrs Macrae's burnt-out car (Picture courtesy of the Scottish* Sun)

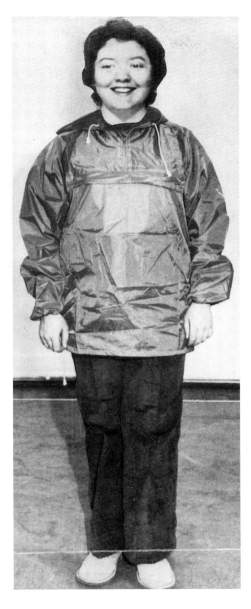

*The Plaza ballroom in Glasgow, where Hilda Miller enjoyed her last night out*

*Agnes Cooney, the children's nurse who may have been the victim of Scotland's forgotten serial killer. This man may also have claimed the lives of at least three other women*

*The Clada Social Club, ten minutes' walk from the Plaza ballroom. Here, Agnes Cooney left her friends after a night out, walked to the city centre – and met her killer*

*Maverick lawyer Willie McRae, found dying with a bullet in his brain in the Highlands in 1985. Was it suicide – or murder? (Picture courtesy of the Scottish* Sun*)*

*The stretch of the Invergarry to Kyle of Lochalsh road, just above Loch Loyne, where Willie McRae may have left the road*

*The cairn erected by friends of Willie McRae to mark the spot where they claim he was murdered*

*Teenager Vicky Hamilton who disappeared while waiting for a
bus to take her from Bathgate to her home near Falkirk. Her body
has never been found and she has not been in contact. Or has she?
(Picture courtesy of the Missing Persons Bureau)*

*Two images of Vicky – one as she was when she disappeared in 1991, the other as she may look now.
The photograph was artificially aged using a photosketch computer by the Missing Persons Bureau
(Picture courtesy of the Missing Persons Bureau)*

# Fife Constabulary

## Death of Alexander 'SANDY' DRUMMOND

HONDA 500 CC. MOTORCYCLE
Reg. mark C358 ASL

BLUE NYLON SPORTS HOLDALL
"G.B. Papers SAFETY AWARD"
on side.

On the evening of Monday 24th June, 1991. The body of ALEXANDER 'SANDY' DRUMMOND, No. 2 Falside Cottage, by Boarhills, near St. Andrews was found on a farm track leading from the main St. Andrews to Kingsbarns Road, (A917) opposite Falside Smithy. The start of the track is located close to the bridge which crosses the Kenly Burn.

The deceased was 33 years old, 5'6" tall, medium build with brown balding hair and when found was wearing a sleeveless denim jacket, yellow 'T' shirt, camouflage trousers and black boots.

It is known that between 3 - 4 p.m. on Friday 21st June, 1991 he visited St. Andrews Town Centre and was seen speaking to a man, aged 20 - 30 years, 5'6" tall. At this time he may well have had his Motor Cycle, pictured and described above with him and was wearing a black leather jerkin.

It is also known that about 11 a.m. on Monday 24th June, 1991 he again visited St. Andrews Town Centre again wearing his leather jacket. Later that afternoon it is thought that he may have revisited St. Andrews as a man fitting his description alighted from the Leven - St. Andrews No. 95 bus in Lamond Drive, St. Andrews.

Police would also like to locate a missing holdall type bag identical to the one pictured above. Such a bag was presented to Sandy, an employee of the Guardbridge Paper Mill. If anyone has recently found such an item or has seen one discarded the Police should be informed.

Anyone with any information about Sandy's movements during the week prior to the finding of his body on the evening of Monday 24th June. 1991 or who has information regarding the identity of the man known to have spoken to him in St. Andrews on Friday 21st June, 1991 is asked to contact Cupar Police Station (Tel. No. Cupar 56070 or 52226) or any Police Station.

WILLIAM McD. MOODIE

*The poster issued by Fife police to help track down Sandy Drummond's killer*
*(Picture courtesy of the Scottish Sun)*

*Arthur Thomson (right), his wife Rita and son Arthur Jnr. Soon the happy family would be fragmented by a gunman's bullets (Picture courtesy of the Scottish Sun)*

*Armed police officers ready for action outside Arthur Thompson's home during a dramatic early morning raid (Picture courtesy of the Scottish Sun)*

*Wreaths decorate the pavement outside the Thompson family home on the morning of Big Arthur's funeral (Picture courtesy of the Scottish Sun)*

*Paul Ferris walks into the sun a free man after being found not guilty of all charges in the High Court of Glasgow (Picture courtesy of the Scottish Sun)*

ities have remained silent about the affair – have refused even to hold a fatal accident inquiry – and so all we can do is study what facts are known. And wonder.

When Willie McRae was first found that Easter Saturday morning nobody knew he had been shot. There was no gun to be seen – it would not be found until two days later, at least 20 feet away, under a small overhang in the burn. Had there been the slightest suspicion that this was anything more than an accident, then it is to be hoped that the first policeman on the scene would not have allowed so many people to trample over the locus, disturbing possible evidence.

When the ambulanceman arrived from Fort William, the onlookers and a police officer helped him heft the body out of the car and into the ambulance, thus destroying what forensic evidence there may have been. The police officer took what has been described as a hold-all – actually, it was a small leather pouch – from the rear seat of the car where it was still apparently sitting beside the flat tyre (even though the car was supposed to have somersaulted down the hill to land facing back in the direction of Invergarry. It also has to be noted that David Coutts does not recall seeing the tyre at that time). The officer asked Coutts to pack McRae's personal items into it. Had they known the man had been shot, these items would have been bagged and tagged and kept for examination. No civilian would have been allowed into or in fact anywhere near the car. The entire area would have been taped off and no police officer would have touched anything until the forensic team had arrived with their polythene bags, tweezers, sticky tape and all the other accoutrements of their trade.

It was while he was gathering the injured man's personal effects that Mr Coutts found a small pile of papers, carefully ripped up and placed in a small bundle about 45 feet away from the car. Among these papers were a credit-card bill, an invoice from a local garage and, inexplicably, McRae's watch face. These items were picked up and put in the hold-all, along with some books, a Bible and a half-empty bottle of whisky, found in the glove compartment and amazingly intact after the supposed accident.

But there was no briefcase and no files. Also, Mr McRae was a chain smoker and had developed a taste for Gold Flake cigarettes before the war. However, after the war they were no longer available in this country and he had to have them specially imported from Eire. But there was no sign of the cigarettes in their distinctive bright yellow packaging. It seems unlikely he would leave for a long weekend without having ensured that he had a proper supply. It could, however, be argued that after his close brush with death the night before in his burning bed he may have resolved to give up smoking, making a start by not taking any with him. But like everything else connected to this case, that is only conjecture. Also missing was a Scottish £100 note which Willie McRae carried with him at all times as a good-luck piece. He had told a restaurant owner with whom he was friendly that it was his first fee as a solicitor. So, if he had these items with him in the first place, it looked as if someone had ransacked the car before anyone else had arrived that morning.

The injured man was rushed to Raigmore hospital in Inverness, where doctors decided that the brain damage was too great for them to treat. He was then transferred to Aberdeen Royal Infirmary, which is standard procedure. The Inverness hospital did not have the necessary equipment to treat a brain-damaged patient. According to the official story, no one had as yet noticed that he was suffering from a gunshot wound. But according to one report, the telephone call from the Inverness hospital to Aberdeen intimated that the man they were sending had a gunshot wound to the head!

Again according to the authorities, it was when he was placed on a life-support machine and X-rays taken that the bullet was discovered still lodged in his brain. It was inoperable, having already destroyed all motor-function capability. At half past three in the afternoon on Sunday 7 April his brother, having taken advice from the consulting neurologist, decided to have the life-support machine switched off and Willie McRae officially died.

The body was then returned to Raigmore hospital in Inverness where a post-mortem was carried out. Although the man had actually died in Grampian Region, he had sustained his injuries in Highland Region. Any inquiry would therefore fall into the jurisdiction of the Inverness procurator fiscal, hence the reason for the post-mortem being carried out there – although the press believed it would be carried out in Aberdeen at the earliest possible opportunity. The results of this examination have never been made public, nor did the family apparently receive a copy. At the time, the Inverness procurator fiscal told the press: 'The death has been fully investigated. There are no suspicious circumstances in this case.' But there are indeed circumstances which are at the very least suspicious.

Although his brother, a doctor, accepted that Willie McRae committed suicide – he broke a long-standing silence about the affair by writing to the *Herald* newspaper in June 1993 saying he was sure the suicide 'was an attempt to save my wife, me and our family from what he perceived was the disgrace of a drunk-driving conviction' – friends have not been quite so confident. Their cynicism has brushed off on many journalists and writers in the nine years since the death.

According to information gleaned by Andrew Murray Scott and Iain MacLeay, the authors of *Britain's Secret War* (Mainstream, 1990), there was no alcohol found in McRae's bloodstream. In short, he had not been drinking before the accident, thus weakening the accident theory. He also knew the road well and it is unlikely he would have spun out of control as he rounded that particular bend. It's sharp, but not that sharp.

When it was discovered that McRae had in fact been shot and was not the victim of a motoring accident, the police returned to the locus and carried out a search for clues. The gun – McRae's own old .22 calibre pistol – was found at least 20 feet away from where the car had been lying. Again, versions of how far away the gun lay differ but most agree that it was too far away to have fallen out of McRae's grasp after he had (allegedly) pulled the trigger.

That was until 1990 when Peter Fraser, Lord Fraser of Carmyllie, who had been solicitor general at the time before becoming Lord Advocate and then Scottish Home Affairs minister, said: 'The revolver was recovered by police on 7 April 1985, from a burn directly below where the driver's door of his car had been. I wish to further emphasise the position of the gun when recovered. It was not found some distance from Mr McRae's car, as has been reported.'

Yet, David Coutts tells of looking under the car when a policeman's hat was blown off and he went to retrieve it. He did not see the gun. Certainly, the area is densely covered with heather and long grass, while the burn itself is very narrow and in parts almost completely covered, but considering the number of people who were around the car at that time – and when the car was winched away – is it likely that everyone failed to notice a pistol? Also, the car was found with the driver's door wedged tightly into the bank of the small burn, so how did the gun end up actually in the water and under an overhang?

Tests showed that only Willie McRae's fingerprints were found on the gun. So if it was found 20 feet away, how did it end up such a distance from the car? One thought was that after he had pulled the trigger, the recoil would have sent it flying out of the open window. The sheer distance made this unlikely and at any rate, if that were the case – and if the gun was found beneath the car – then surely he would have been found with his arm lying outside the window and not with his hands folded on his lap? Another theory was that the gun had somehow bounced from the grass and rocks to where it was finally found. This is not just unlikely, but ludicrous

There is a slim possibility that McRae himself threw it there, although again it is highly unlikely. Forensic scientist Professor John Glaister wrote that 'even after a serious injury has been sustained, the injured man or woman may still be capable of performing certain actions before death'. To illustrate this, Professor Glaister told a story concerning an elderly man shot in the head with a Colt .45 pistol. The bullet entered under the chin and passed through both the frontal and temporal lobes of the brain. Death or at least unconsciousness should have been instantaneous but the wounded man could still walk a short distance to his hotel, where he not only spoke to a servant but also hung up his brolly, took off his overcoat and walked down a flight of stairs to the bathroom where he finally collapsed and died. However, medical opinion regarding Willie McRae stated the bullet had rendered any motor functions impossible immediately.

Friends of the dead man believe he was murdered, perhaps by drug smugglers in the Highlands with whom he apparently had a running feud. Not only did he object to the nuclear industry poisoning his country, he objected to these people bringing substances which could poison the populace in through the quiet bays and inlets near his west-coast home.

The principal suspects, however, are agents of the state who, the theory goes, murdered McRae to prevent him from making any further trouble for the nuclear industry, or because of his nationalist sympathies, or because of his alleged connections to the fugitives David Dinsmore and Adam Busby. Advocates of the assassination theory cite the case of Hilda Murrell as corroborative evidence that the state will silence anyone who becomes too troublesome. The elderly English rosegrower, nuclear protester and vociferous critic of the decision to sink the *Belgrano* during the Falklands war was found dead in woods near her home, which had in turn been broken into and papers rifled. Two books concerning the case have been written which state strongly that she was murdered by the security services.

Curiously, author Graham Swift had his home broken into and searched while he was writing his book on the case, *Death of a Rosegrower*. Willie McRae had also mentioned to friends that his cottage in Dornie had been broken into several times and what papers he kept there gone through. His Glasgow home was broken into in 1984 with nothing taken.

Witnesses had reported seeing a red Ford Escort several times in the vicinity of Hilda Murrell's home. By coincidence, a red Ford Escort figures, albeit tenuously, in the Willie McRae story. About an hour before McRae's body was discovered, a group of hill walkers at Creag Bhan on Loch Eilt, about 50 miles from the scene of the 'accident', said they were fired upon by a man with a high-powered rifle who had climbed out of a red Ford Escort. Fifty miles away may not seem that far, especially if it is travelled in a fast car. But Loch Eilt can only be reached from the Loch Loyne area via a series of narrow, twisting roads. What would a gunman be doing on the road to Mallaig? Unless his escape plan included a boat hidden in one of the many secluded coves on the west coast.

Then there were the comments made by an anonymous police officer connected to what the authorities somewhat laughably called an inquiry into the case, ordered over two months later. He told a reporter on the *Sunday Mail* that although McRae's gun had been fired twice, he was not shot at point-blank range – and the rear window seemed to have been shattered by a bullet.

So was he shot at point-blank range? In 1990 Lord Fraser wrote in a letter to Sir Nicholas Fairbairn, MP for Perth and Kinross, that the post-mortem had shown that the pistol had been pressed firmly against the skin. If so, then there are certain signs which must have been present. There are three types of gunshot wounds which we have to consider here – contact wounds, intermediate-range wounds and long-range wounds.

If Willie McRae shot himself then the wound would be a contact wound. If he held the barrel of the pistol hard against his temple and pulled the trigger, the edges of the bullet hole may be burnt by the flammable gases which erupt from the muzzle of the gun. Soot would be also be indelibly imprinted on the surrounding skin – the further away the muzzle of the gun is, the area of soot widens but the density lessens. If there is bone under the entry wound, then the gasses from the muzzle may well cause the overlying flesh to tear into a messy star-shaped wound. Black powder from the old ammunition used could also be present but this could have been easily washed off in hospital. If he held the gun only lightly against his head, then the soot would not be embedded but there would be a band formed around the wound. No one, neither the people who carried him from the car to the ambulance, nor the nurses who without a doubt would have cleaned him in hospital, saw – or have mentioned seeing – such traces. But then, his head was covered in blood at the locus – and if the bullet hole was not discovered at Raigmore then the staff would not have seen them. But nurses at Aberdeen told researchers later that they did not see such traces either.

In intermediate-range wounds, where the gun is held between two to eight inches away, an effect called 'tattooing' may be seen. This is caused by particles of burned powder being forced under the skin – particles which cannot be washed away. Hot muzzle gases also cause an area of burning around the skin known as the 'scorch zone'. Again no one has reported seeing such marks.

As for long-range wounds, they show neither powder nor soot deposits, the only mark on the body being that of the entry wound. So if Willie McRae was shot through the rear window of his car – as the unnamed police officer said – then the entry wound would obviously be at the back of the head. Blood loss at the entrance of long-range wounds can often be slight as the hole tends to close up behind the bullet as it forces its way through. Most of the visible damage is caused when the bullet exits. Could it be in this case that there was a second wound at the back of the head, with the blood on McRae's forehead coming from the exit wound at the front? A nurse was said to have seen X-rays which confirmed there were two wounds but this may well have been pictures of the same wound taken from two different angles. But the official reports state that the bullet was found lodged in the brain. And if the wound on the front of the head was a contact wound, then it would not be as neat as a long-range or even intermediate wound. It would also bleed substantially. Again, without access to the post-mortem, we cannot know for sure what was found. Or what was not found.

But if McRae was murdered and his death made to look like suicide, why did the killer throw the gun so far away? Surely he would have known it would have excited interest?

Questions. Questions. And very few of them have answers.

Why have the authorities consistently refused to conduct a fatal accident inquiry? Almost three months after the incident, Thomas Aitchieson, the Inverness procurator fiscal, announced that further inquiries were to be made because there were some facets of the case which required further investigation. 'I admit I said there were no suspicious circumstances,' he said, 'but I have been investigating this ever since. I sent a report to the Crown Office but they have put it back in my court. I can give no details.' He also said that there were 'all sorts of factors coming into this', 'all sorts of stories being put out'. But he could not comment on them. No details. No comment. It was all becoming so depressingly familiar.

It was said at the time that the decision not to hold a fatal accident inquiry was made after consultation with both the dead man's relatives and the hierarchy of the Scottish National Party who all agreed that such an inquiry was not necessary. Later, Peter Fraser, now Lord Fraser of Carmyllie but then still only the solicitor general, announced: 'I personally took the decision that there should be no fatal accident inquiry. This is not unusual where the circumstances, so far as ascertained, reveal no criminality on the part of another person known or unknown.' Unsurprisingly, he added: 'I am not in a position to elaborate on my reasoning.'

No criminality? What is the theft of files and money from an injured man if not evidence of criminality? No matter which way you look at it, the wrong decision seems to have been taken. William McRae was a well-known and well-respected political and legal figure. Something more than a superficial investigation was called for by friends. And they are still calling for it. But the powers that be are not listening.

Even Winnie Ewing, the doyenne of SNP members, seemed to detect the strong odour of fish lingering around the case. At the request of party members, she conducted an internal inquiry, predictably being refused access to the official reports and photographs. Eventually, she had to tell the national executive committee: 'I regret therefore that I cannot, as I hoped to, say to the national executive commit-tee that I am satisfied that Willie did commit suicide.' And there the matter stands. The conspiracy, if conspiracy there is, has been successful. No official investigation has ever been carried out.

Of course, there have been unofficial inquiries, by Winnie Ewing, journalists, writers and, in particular, John Conway, a retired forensic scientist who spent years working in Belfast and who was living in Nairn when McRae died. Mr Conway is no conspiracy theorist but he believes strongly that certain people knew about the bullet wound from the beginning. He says that stories of a man being shot above Loch Loyne were being discussed in the British Legion club in Nairn and in Inverness pubs on the Saturday night – two days before the authorities announced it. He has made studies of the area and also 'done a lot of digging' and is in no doubt that McRae met his death at the hands of security agents. He believes it was a two-car ambush, one car following him, the other driving towards him and forcing him off the road. He was shot as he lay unconscious in the driver's seat. 'It was a small wound, just a small hole,' he said. 'It wasn't until they cut the hair back in the hospital to examine it that they realised it looked like a bullet hole. This was confirmed when they took an X-ray.' If that is true, so much then for the contact-wound scenario. The inquiry which followed was a half-hearted one, he believes. 'They did not even speak to the missionary cou-ple Willie McRae had supper with that evening,' he points out. He claims that the security services 'deliberately muddy the waters' in cases such as this. 'That way, no one can see the bottom of the pond,' he says. The retired scientist has written a book entitled *To Speak for the Dead* which details his inves-tigations into the McRae case as well as five other mysterious deaths, including that of Hilda Murrell and John McLennan, a police officer found dead with five stab wounds in his body. At the time of writing he is still looking for a publisher.

It is clear now that the Willie McRae case will not go away. Michael Strathern has formed the Willie McRae Society, dedicated to making public what they believe is the truth about his death. They have been hampered, they believe, by nameless and faceless people in Whitehall who have swept so many things under the carpet they have to walk uphill to get to their desk. Every year on the anniversary of his friend's death, Michael Strathern and his supporters meet at a cairn built on a lay-by above what they believe is the scene of the murder and hold a memorial service.

But is it the correct site? Others, including David Coutts, disagree. They believe the real locus was over one mile south, in Lochaber district. Mr Coutts points out that you can see the dam at the end of Loch Loyne from the 'official' site, but he does not remember being able to see the dam on that wet spring morning in 1985. The two groups have agreed to differ over the point, but David Coutts did write to the Inverness procurator fiscal for clarification. He did not receive a reply. The society's site certainly bears all the landmarks: there is a small stream flooding from a culvert under the road and a sharp bend in the road. It is also more accessible to the public, having a much larger lay-by than the so-called Coutts site. In the end though, it does not matter exactly where Mr McRae died, only that there are questions regarding the death.

Beside the cairn grows a clump of thistle, a touch by nature of which Willie McRae would no doubt have approved. The wind whistles through the tough grass growing on the hillside. Down the valley, the shades of higher hills and peaks can be seen looming through the misty rain, backlit by sunlight. And on a small plaque near the foot of the pile of rubble there are the words:

WILLIE McRAE
'A SCOTTISH PATRIOT'
DIED HERE 6TH APRIL 1985
'THE STRUGGLE GOES ON'

In life, Willie McRae was a thorn in their side. In death, he appears to be the entire rosebush.

# MISSING

THE FACE ON the poster looks familiar. Dark hair, bobbed and neatly combed, framing a young face and a shy smile. The collar and tie and dark jumper of what looks like a school uniform. And the girl's name, dimly remembered from the newspaper coverage.

Then there is the other photograph. She looks older than her 15 years in this one but she has perhaps been caught shortly after getting out of bed. It is an informal snap, taken one Christmas, and she is still wearing her dressing-gown, a box of half-unwrapped chocolates on her lap, her hair, although in roughly the same style as the other photograph, is tousled. There is no bashful smile in this picture. She looks, somehow, haunted. Or perhaps it is merely the look any teenage girl gives while being photographed when looking far from her best.

The posters stare down from police-station walls all over Central Scotland and beyond. They are placed on noticeboards beside the front desk, where the public can walk in and look and read the terse text beside the picture. And remember . . .

At first the reports in the press were small, merely recording the fact that 15-year-old Vicky Fay Hamilton was missing. She had been seen last on Sunday, 10 February 1991, in Bathgate bus station, asking about buses back to her home near Falkirk. She was described as 5 foot 5 inches in height, of medium build, with brown eyes, short black dyed hair and wearing denims, a black bomber jacket with bright orange reversible lining, a grey sweatshirt with UNISYS in red letters and brown shoes. She was carrying a black handbag and a sports bag containing clothing. That was all they said in the early days, just after she disappeared. The reports told the readers very little about a girl they would soon come to know very well, without ever actually meeting her. Her face would become as familiar as their own daughters' through exposure on television and newspapers.

But all that would come later. For now, there was nothing to distinguish her disappearance from any of the others we read about practically every day. Experts say that around 250,000 people vanish in Britain every single year. They can only estimate the figure because, as yet, there are no statistics kept. In 1991, 8,341 people went missing in Strathclyde alone; over half were in their teens. They disappear for a variety of reasons – arguments with parents, despair over broken relationships, problems at school, drug addiction, in a small number of cases to escape sexually and physically abusive relatives, and to an even lesser degree, abduction. Most of them turn up within a few days, either back home or at the homes of friends or relatives. In a very few cases, they gravitate to London, lured by the belief that they will find quick and easy money there and the knowledge that they can slip easily into the big city crowds. What too many of them find is a bed in a shop doorway or a pimp who will hook them on drugs and send them out on to the streets. Increasingly now, it is the male teenage runaways who wind up taking this route, more often than not being targeted within 24 hours of hitting the city.

But Vicky Hamilton would not be found on the street corners of London although there have been unsubstantiated claims that she has been spotted in the King's Cross and Paddington areas. Vicky Hamilton is one of the tiny percentage of missing persons who just seem to disappear without trace, in her case leaving behind heartbroken relatives, already split by family problems. Police officers, after taking thousands of statements and following up just as many lines of inquiry, finally admitted to being baffled. And police officers do not like to admit failure.

Ultimately, there is not much the police can do once the initial searches have taken place. If the missing person is under age then they will pull out all the stops to find the child. If the missing person is an adult and there is no sign of foul play, then they cannot take the matter much further. In general, they cannot – do not – spend much time helping the relatives come to terms with what has happened.

Janet Newman, one of the founders of the Missing Persons Bureau, a London-based charity which has grown swiftly in size and influence since its beginnings three years ago as an experiment in Bristol, says they are there to help people who are left behind – and if that means trying to locate the missing person then that is what they do. The bureau has a 75 percent success rate in finding missing persons. Janet herself has been deeply involved in trying to locate Vicky Hamilton – and may even have spoken to her.

Vicky was a typical 15-year-old girl. She liked music and was devoted to her dog. She was a daddy's girl, often visiting her father, Michael, at his new home. He had divorced her mother, Janette, but lived not far from her in the small village of Redding, near Falkirk, with his new wife, Christine. Vicky lived with her mother and her young brother and sister, the twins Lindsay and Lee. Her older sister, Sharon, had already left home and was staying in her own house in Livingston, the rapidly sprawling new town on the road to Edinburgh.

On the weekend she vanished, the schoolgirl had been visiting her sister. On Sunday, 10 February 1991, Vicky phoned her mother in Redding to tell her she was about to leave and make her way home. It was just before five in the afternoon and it was the last time Janette Hamilton would ever speak to her daughter.

The girl caught a bus to Bathgate, arriving there at about 5.20 p.m. She intended to catch a second bus there to take her on the final leg home, a bus, as far as is known, she never caught. Vicky was unsure of the journey. Her father would normally have collected her from her sister's house and driven her back to Redding, but on this particular weekend his road tax had run out and he had not wanted to risk being stopped by the police. She had asked the driver of the bus from Livingston to let her know when she was in the centre of Bathgate and, once there, nervously asked a few people about what bus would take her home. The ground was covered with eight inches of snow that dark Sunday evening so when she found that she had time to kill before her next bus, Vicky bought herself a bag of chips from Valente's fish and chip shop in Bathgate's main square, known locally as the Steelyard, to ward off the bitter cold. The chip shop and the video store were the only businesses open at the time but both were doing a brisk trade and a number of people were milling around the square. Many of them remembered seeing the girl sitting alone on a bench near the chip shop, eating her food. Once she had eaten her chips, it was time to make her way to the bus stop. On the way, she stopped again, this time outside a car-accessory shop to ask someone if she was on the right road. She was and she went on her way. And that, as far as is known for certain, was the last time she was seen.

Janette Hamilton, stuck in the house looking after her young children, had asked a friend to meet Vicky's bus at the other end, in Redding. When the teenager did not step off that bus, or any other bus that night, the police were contacted. And so the search began, a search that, for some people, has never really ended. At its height it would involve officers from three police forces, making it the biggest hunt of its kind ever seen in West Lothian. But then, such hunts are always the biggest things seen in their particular area. Newspapers covered the search closely and even BBC TV's *Crimewatch UK* eventually became involved. But Vicky Hamilton has eluded them all.

Bathgate and the surrounding area were searched thoroughly by over 150 police officers, some with tracker dogs, others with specially trained search-and-rescue dogs used during the horrific and heartrending Lockerbie disaster. The search teams were controlled from a special incident room set up in Bathgate police office. Naturally, police were not working on the assumption that any harm had come to the girl, although this could not have been ruled out. There was the possibility that she had decided to start walking home for some reason, had grown tired and decided to rest somewhere.

She could have been lying along the road, in a barn, under a bush perhaps, suffering from exposure.

Police officers walked the roads between Bathgate and Falkirk, looking in the barns and under the bushes, checking stretches of wasteland, fields and woods. Mounted police combed the rougher ground, their dark silhouettes often seen moving silently across the stark winter skyline. Officers picked their way through the rubble of derelict buildings while an RAF search-and-rescue helicopter swooped and darted in the skies above, keeping in radio contact with the ground search patrols below. Meanwhile, an underwater team explored rivers, ponds and streams. The depths of disused mines were also plumbed. People living in outlying areas were asked to search outbuildings and barns. In Bathgate, officers began house-to-house inquiries, knocking on doors, asking the occupants if they had seen the girl, or spoken to her, or helped her in any way. But they found nothing; not a clue; not a trace; not a shred of clothing.

'This girl cannot just have vanished into thin air,' one perplexed police officer told reporters. 'I've never seen a search of this scale before and if she is here we will find her.' But hopes of finding her alive faded with the sun at the end of each desperate day. Janette Hamilton never gave up hope, though. She could not accept that some harm could have befallen her daughter, always believing she would receive some word, a letter, a phone call, anything that would confirm Vicky was alive and well. And so in the early days she seldom moved far from the phone, anxiously waiting for the good news.

But within two weeks of the girl's disappearance, her father had decided he would never see her again. 'No matter what I think or what people tell me I should think,' he told Glasgow's *Evening Times*, 'I still keep coming back to the same conclusion and that is that I will never see Vicky again. I pray I am wrong but deep down I don't think I am. She is not the type of girl to wander off and she would not go with anyone she did not know. Not by her own free will.'

But sightings of the girl flooded in, from Bathgate, from Falkirk, even from Ayrshire. Each one was carefully investigated by police officers but each one yielded nothing. Detectives travelled on the no. 218 Craighill to Bathgate bus – the bus the girl took from her sister's house – in the hope they would find passengers who remembered seeing her. They flooded the Steelyard with officers. Some witnesses recalled seeing a young girl climbing into a taxi there between 5.40 p.m. and 6.15 p.m. so police issued appeals to any taxi driver who may have picked the girl up in Bathgate on the night she disappeared. They particularly wanted to speak to a taxi driver who collected two girls on Friday 8 February in Livingston or Uphall. One of these girls may have been Vicky. They also wished to speak to the other girl, whoever she was. But that line of inquiry, like so many others, led nowhere.

Then, just as they despaired of ever finding a clue, Vicky's purse was found in Edinburgh. It was seen sticking out from under a workman's hut at the side of the pavement in St Andrew Square, very near to the city's central bus station, on Thursday 21 February. A workman retrieved it and handed it in to the police, who promptly sent it off for forensic testing.

The purse contained the ticket for her last bus journey, as well as a few cards, telephone numbers and personal items. It only held five pence in cash, and police told reporters it had been known that the girl had just enough money in her purse to get from Bathgate to Edinburgh by bus, but not by taxi. Unless she had money no one else knew about; not her mother, not her father, not her sister. Detectives were of the opinion that the purse had been thrown away in St Andrew Square and had not lain there longer than one night. The question was, why? And, of course, by whom? Did the young girl throw it there herself, purposely ditching a tangible memory of the life she intended to leave behind? Or was it disposed of by someone else? There was, however, still no sign of her turquoise sports bag.

There was a theory that Vicky was worried about coming out of hiding because she was fearful of repercussions. The sheer scale of the hunt may have been keeping her underground because she was worried about what would happen to her if she reappeared after causing so much trouble. The police issued statements to the press designed to reassure her that there would be no action taken if she just went home, or merely got in touch with her parents or a police office. But there was no word from Vicky. Or anyone claiming to be her. Not yet, anyway. Meanwhile, there were further sightings, over 70 of them, in Falkirk, Bathgate and Edinburgh. Naturally, each one of them was carefully checked out. Each one of them had to be carefully checked out. Each one of them came to nothing.

By this time, the girl had been missing for over two weeks and police decided it was time to recreate her last known movements in a bid to jog the memories of existing witnesses and unearth new ones. A policewoman who matched the girl's height and rough description was found and on Sunday 3 March, exactly three weeks after Vicky's disappearance, wearing similar clothes, she followed the missing girl's route from Livingston to Bathgate, where she got off the bus, bought chips at Valente's fish and chip shop, sat on the same bench and then walked off towards the bus stop. As she was doing this, police officers stopped passers-by and asked them if they had seen a similarly dressed girl three weeks before and if they had, had she spoken to them and which way did she go.

The reconstruction was deemed a success, bringing in more information about what the girl did and who she spoke to in Bathgate town centre. They found the people from whom she had asked directions to the bus stop while the staff at the chip shop remembered her sitting outside. And witnesses remembered something very important, giving the police a fresh lead to work on.

They recalled seeing a large white car – either an old Ford Cortina or Ford Granada Mark 4 – in a small carpark on the south side of South Bridge station, near the bus station at around six p.m. The car had its headlights on and the windows appeared to be steamed up. One witness had come forward saying that Vicky had been seen asking the male driver for directions to the bus stop. Who was this driver? And had he offered the girl a lift? And, if so, what happened during the drive? Although a number of appeals were issued to this man to come forward, he was never traced, leaving these questions unanswered and detectives and the girl's family even more frustrated.

They had more luck with customers of the Clydesdale Bank who had used the autobank facility in the square. The bank wrote to customers who had used the cash dispenser at or near the time the girl had been in the square. The customers came forward, many confirming they had seen her.

The police also confirmed that the Samaritans had received a call from a mystery man ten days after the girl disappeared who said that the missing girl was 'okay'. The caller, however, was very vague and rang off before any details could be obtained. Detectives followed up what they could from what little the man said – full details of which have never been released – and urged him to call again. But there was no further word from him.

By 20 March the ground search had ended. They had covered every inch of land they could in and around Bathgate and were confident that Vicky was not in the area. But the inquiry itself was not to be wound down. They had no way of knowing then, but they would be back on the same ground within a month.

Before that though, the not inconsiderable power of television came into play with an item on BBC TV's influential *Crimewatch UK*. The programme did not normally handle missing-person cases – its remit runs more to murder and other serious crimes – but the makers agreed to include an item on the Vicky Hamilton case because of the increasing police concern for the youngster's safety. Additional phone lines were installed in the incident room in Bathgate to help handle the expected flood of information. In the end, that flood turned out to be only a trickle with just four calls being received before the end of the programme which was aired on Thursday, 11 April 1991. However, as time went on, it generated a further 60 sightings from as far away as London, Aberdeen and Yorkshire.

Two female detectives travelled south to liaise with experts in the Metropolitan Police's juvenile protection unit. They intended to visit all the places in London which acted as meeting places for runaway youngsters. But nothing new was found, at either the new sightings or in London.

Then police search teams found themselves back out in open ground. And this time they were looking for a body. Another anonymous male caller had contacted the police. This man claimed that he had killed Vicky and dumped her corpse in a lay-by in the Bathgate area. The proposed search area extended to an eight-mile radius around the town, overlapping not only Lothian and Borders Region, but also Central and Strathclyde. Officers from each of these police forces mounted an exhaustive search along the miles of country roads, checking not only lay-bys but also woods, quarries and fields. They had combed many of them before but they were going to do it again. 'We will search for as long as it takes,' said one senior officer, predicting that it would take up to a fortnight to complete a full search of the area. However, the inquiry was still not being treated as murder. Anonymous calls have to be taken seriously, one officer said, but there was still no evidence that the girl was dead. Secretly, though, some senior officers suspected that the girl had come to some harm. The search sparked off by the cruel hoax uncovered nothing new. Vicky Hamilton's family, waiting anxiously for further news, experienced another disappointment. They did not wish Vicky to be found dead, but not knowing what happened to her was equally as upsetting.

Then the girl – or someone claiming to be her – got in touch. Wednesday 24 April was Vicky Hamilton's 16th birthday and on that day a young girl phoned a Radio Forth programme with a message to Janette Hamilton, telling her that she was alive and well. 'Someone tell my mum I'm fine and to stop worrying,' said the voice. The same person phoned Broxburn police station the following day with the same message. No one knows if it was Vicky or yet another crank delighting in a fake message. But if it was Vicky, Detective Chief Inspector Bill Crookston, spearheading the hunt, urged her to call again. 'If it is Vicky I would appeal to her to keep in contact,' he said. 'She is now 16 years old and if she does not want her location disclosed I shall respect that. But I have to see her face to face.' Perhaps the call was a hoax, like many another already received and still to be received. Or perhaps it really was the missing girl, now legally of an age to do what she wanted but not wishing to speak directly to her mother. She would – or someone like her – be heard from again.

The investigation began to wind down. The officers returned from London with nothing new to report although a woman had phoned saying that she was sharing a flat with Vicky and the two of them were working as prostitutes in the city's West End. The call had come soon after the Scottish detectives had spoken to prostitutes in the King's Cross area, distributing pictures of the girl. As usual, the woman did not get in touch again and the officers could find no trace of Vicky among London's vice girls. But that does not mean she was – *is* – not there. All leads had been exhausted and there were no fresh clues to work on. By the end of July, the number of officers working on the case had been halved. As time went on, it would be reduced further still, until only one officer was responsible for checking any fresh information.

Janette Hamilton, however, had still refused to give up hope. She was disappointed but, as she told the *Daily Record*: 'I'm still praying my daughter is alive and well somewhere.' That Christmas, the grieving mother could not bring herself to buy a present for her missing daughter. 'Vicky always loved Christmas,' she told the *Record*. 'She was the life and soul of the party every year. Now the place will seem empty without her. It's not going to be a happy Christmas in our house.' Janette intended to spend the day quietly with her seven-year-old twins, Lee and Lindsay. Naturally, she would make the festive season as enjoyable for them as possible but her thoughts, she said, were with Vicky. 'I thought about buying a present for Vicky but I can't bring myself to do it,' she said. She would, instead, put some money into a building society account in case the girl came home.

But she never came home. And her mother never gave up

hope. She spoke regularly to police officers involved in the search. She was always willing to talk to journalists about her daughter, to do anything to keep the case – and Vicky's memory – alive. She kept in contact with the Missing Persons Bureau, which runs a 24-hour helpline for worried relatives of missing persons. The anxious mother would often phone Janet Newman in the early hours of the morning, just to talk to someone. 'I remember one night she phoned me to ask if I thought she should move the photograph of Vicky from the mantelpiece to a drawer,' recalled Janet Newman. 'She said that every time she walked past it or looked at it she felt ghastly. I pointed out that even in a drawer she would feel the same thing because she knew the photograph was there. I think she desperately needed someone to talk to.'

Mrs Hamilton even travelled down to London to meet with Diana Lamplugh, the mother of estate agent Suzy Lamplugh, who disappeared at the age of 25 in 1986 after arranging to meet the mysterious Mr Kipper. Mrs Lamplugh had set up the Suzy Lamplugh Trust, an organisation which supports the parents of missing children and Janette Hamilton had planned to set up a similar group in Scotland. She prayed constantly that her daughter would walk through her front door, smiling and saying she was back to stay. But further tragedy was waiting round the corner.

By the end of 1992, the months of stress and uncertainty had taken their toll on Janette Hamilton. On Hogmanay, she collapsed and had to be taken into hospital with fluid in her lungs. On Tuesday, 12 January 1993, her heart gave out and she died in Falkirk's Royal Infirmary. She was only 41 years of age. Over 100 mourners attended her funeral at Muiravonside cemetery, Linthlithgow. As slivers of sleet sliced down from a slate-coloured sky, Sharon Hamilton, Vicky's 22-year-old sister, and her eight-year-old brother each placed a single red rose on their mother's coffin. They were watched by other members of the family – including Michael, Vicky's father, and senior police officers as well as the man who had led the hunt for Vicky, DCI Bill Crookston, now retired from the force. In August 1993, Sharon married and announced that she was to adopt the twins. It is an unusual step in Scotland but one she obviously thought necessary for the children's own well-being.

In February 1993, new pictures were released along with a new appeal in *The Big Issue*, the magazine written for and by the homeless which contains a page inserted by the Missing Persons Bureau. A previous appeal in the magazine had brought results – although had not taken the police any closer to finding the girl – and it was thought that on the second anniversary of her disappearance another appeal would not go amiss. This time, though, the picture of the girl was altered. A number of previous sightings had been reported of a girl looking like Vicky but now with blonde hair.

The Missing Persons Bureau also used techniques perfected by the FBI to produce a new picture of Vicky as she might look at the age of 18. The picture was produced on a photo-sketch computer developed by the FBI to help them track down criminals who had been on the run for some time. The £30,000 image enhancer has been given to the Missing Persons Bureau by contacts in the USA and is the only one of its kind, and with the only trained operator, in Europe. They use it not only to age photographs of people who have been missing for some time, but also to build up faces which have been obscured in snaps. The new image of Vicky was published in the 3 July 1993 edition of the *Weekend Times*, the magazine-style Saturday edition of Glasgow's *Evening Times*. But still there is no trace of the girl.

Janet Newman is convinced she is still alive and living in London. In fact, she may even have talked to her. Just before Christmas 1992, the Missing Persons Bureau collaborated in the making of a television programme with a London company. Broadcast only in the London area, the programme was a *Crimewatch*-style show, with one of the items concerning the search for Vicky Hamilton. Janette Hamilton was taken to London to appear.

Nine months later, a further three hour-long programmes were broadcast, this time on the ITV network. Although the Vicky Hamilton case only featured briefly in the final programme, a huge blow-up of her photograph was displayed prominently on the backdrop of the set. During the course of the three-week run, a girl phoned the special hot-line four times, saying she was Vicky, from what she said obviously unaware that her mother was dead. The final call was taken by Janet Newman herself. 'The voice came on the line and said she was Vicky Hamilton and that she was all right but did not want to be found,' she said. 'She said we were to tell her mother she loved her but wanted to be left alone. I asked her to stay on the line so I could confirm she was Vicky but she hung up.' The voice, Janet says, was soft spoken with traces of a Scottish accent. She feels instinctively that it was Vicky.

If that caller was the missing girl, then she is grown up now, perhaps living with someone or married, maybe even with children of her own. Her wish to be left alone must be respected, although Janet wishes she would at least get in touch with her sister or father, to assure them she is all right.

But if that person was not Vicky – and the call just another cruel hoax – then we must address the possibility that she may be dead. And if that is the case, then how did she die? Did someone murder her on that freezing cold night in February? If so, where is her body? The ground was frozen solid, preventing anyone from digging a makeshift grave. Police theories that a body would be found by summer walkers or ramblers have so far not come to pass. And why did the killer – if there was a killer – throw the girl's purse away in Edinburgh? Was this an attempt to send the police on a false trail, to give the killer more time to cover his or her tracks? Or was this done by Vicky herself, perhaps symbolically throwing away her old life as she set off on a new one?

Janet Newman says it is possible to leave an old life behind and start afresh. But you would have to be pretty desperate. 'If you really are that desperate to get away from something, then you can disappear, start up again,' she said. 'But you have to be on the edge of everything, feel there is no way you can turn, nothing else you can do. And you have to be prepared to let your standards of living drop, live in bed-

and-breakfast accommodation perhaps, take menial, low-paying jobs, or live and work on the streets. It's hard, but it can be done.'

She continued: 'It's heartbreaking for the people they leave behind. They can't understand what has happened to them. Some of them – including Janette Hamilton – can think and talk about nothing else.'

So, if Vicky did run away purposely, what happened in her life that made her need to do so? And who was in that car with the steamed-up windows in Bathgate? Was Vicky in there with the driver? And did he take her somewhere and then kill her? Or was he party to her flight from the past?

Janette Hamilton went to her grave hoping her daughter was alive, unable to grieve properly through uncertainty. Janet Newman believes her death was caused partly by a broken heart. Michael Hamilton is convinced his daughter is dead, yet he keeps her photograph pinned up at the front of the coach he drives, just in case someone recognises her. The police remain cautious. The case will always be live, they say, and is still that of a missing person, not murder. They have no evidence that she came to any harm, although many of the officers would admit privately that they believe the girl to be dead.

Perhaps one day the mystery will be solved. It is not unusual for something to come to light a considerable time afterwards. The case of Craig Swann is an example. The 30-year-old mature student vanished from his home in Livingston in August 1992 and it was not until July 1993 that his murdered body was found in a remote wood in Perthshire.

And in another case, a 12-year-old girl from the Lanarkshire town of Coatbridge disappeared in 1957. The case slipped into local legend and remained a mystery. Then, 35 years later the police announced that they were re-opening investigations and it looked as if the puzzle had been solved. Or had it . . . ?

Pretty, twelve-year-old Moira Anderson was highly excited all that day, Saturday, 23 February 1957. That was the day she was being allowed to go to the pictures on her own for the first time. Well, not on her own exactly. She was going to see *Guys and Dolls* that afternoon at the Regal with two cousins, one of whom was 15 years of age. But she was going without her parents for the first time and that was near enough on her own. She often went to the Saturday morning children's club at the Odeon, but this was different, this was the proper pictures. The idea of this trip made her feel so grown up and she was looking forward to it enormously.

But before her big day, her parents had a number of errands for her. First, she went with her father, who had one leg, to the Limb Centre in Motherwell. When she got back to her home at 71 Eglinton Street, Coatbridge, just after 11 a.m., there were other messages for her to run. She did not mind – it just brought her trip to the cinema all that closer.

Then she was told that her outing would have to be postponed to the early evening performance because her older cousin had to visit their sick grandfather in Glasgow's Royal Infirmary. Her grandmother was also ill but she was still at home, in nearby 209 Muiryhall Street. She was not alone – Moira's uncle was staying there – but the girl was still sent round to her granny to see if there was anything she needed.

The youngster left her own home at 3.50 p.m., walking through a fierce snowstorm, arriving at her granny's a few minutes later. As soon as she arrived, her uncle, who was in the kitchen frying some fish for tea, asked her to nip out to the Co-operative grocers on Laird Street for some butter. She was a helpful child and she said she would. Normally, she would have taken her grandmother's collie, Glen, with her. But the weather outside was too ferocious, so he was left, warm and comfortable, lying in front of the fire. Anyway, she would only be gone for a few minutes. But a lot can happen in a few minutes. Decisions can be made, actions can be taken. Had she taken the dog, she might still be alive today.

The young girl shouted something to her granny in the bedroom and then stepped out again into the blizzard. She had three shillings and sixpence in her pocket and her granny's Co-operative order book in her hand. Her fawn-coloured kilted burberry coat was firmly buttoned around her

121

to keep out the snow which was being driven almost horizontally by the howling wind. Underneath her coat a blue scarf kept the winter chill from her young chest and throat and beneath that she wore a blue jumper and lemon-coloured cardigan. She was also wearing a thick tweed skirt, fawn socks and brown shoes. Her short fair hair was encased in a navy-blue woollen pixie hat with red bands. Her mother had ensured that she was properly dressed for the winter weather. She had protected her daughter in every way she could. But the successive layers of clothing could not protect the youngster from everything.

Her family never saw her again. It was as if she had been swallowed up by the swiftly falling snow. Wherever Moira Anderson went that day, it was not to the Co-op in Laird Street, little more than 500 yards from her granny's house. An assistant in the store questioned later knew the girl and was adamant he had not seen her. When Moira did not return to her grandmother's it was at first assumed that she had gone straight on to the pictures. But her cousins had not seen her – and when she had not returned home by 11 that night, the police were called.

And so began a search for a little girl whose disappearance has become part of a town's folklore. The police and hundreds of local volunteers, and at various points of the search striking dustmen as well as Scouts and Rover cubs, saturated the area. Cinema managers were contacted early on Sunday morning to see if she had been locked in by accident. Every park in Coatbridge and nearby Airdrie was searched thoroughly, especially Dunbeth Park which she would have passed to get to the Co-op. Schools and libraries were opened to see if she had managed to get inside. The public were asked to unlock their garages and lock-ups. Search parties scrambled over snow-covered slag heaps and stumbled down muddy mine-shafts. But there was no sign of the young girl.

Eventually, news of the inevitable sightings came in. She was seen on a bus with a man going to Glasgow. She was seen in Greenock and Port Glasgow, one woman there describing her so exactly that it was felt she could not have been mistaken and police rushed down to the Clydeside town fully expecting to find her. They were disappointed. They were always disappointed.

There were the usual sightings from all over the country, most of them ultimately discounted by the police. A family reported seeing a girl answering her description at a funfair in Queen's Park recreation grounds on the south side of Glasgow. But detectives questioning the showpeople got no further. Another sighting in nearby St Andrew's Drive also proved inconclusive as did reports of Moira being seen in Kinning Park, Glasgow. A lorry driver even saw a girl answering her description standing beside two parked lorries outside Doncaster in the north of England. The man, from Dagenham in Essex, was shown a picture of the missing girl and he said: 'It's an awfully good likeness of the girl I saw.' But the girl he saw, whoever she was, was not traced. A railwayman found a blue gaberdine belt hooked on a fence which skirted a local marsh known as The Moss. He handed it to police but Andrew Anderson, Moira's father, said it was not his daughter's. Nevertheless, the marsh was fully searched. Someone called the police, telling them they had seen a young girl being dragged into a van at Baillieston, only four miles away from Coatbridge. The van was chased on the Carlisle Road and stopped at Gretna where it was found that the 'girl' was a young woman who had been hitching a lift.

Moira's parents were convinced their little girl had not run away. The Sunday after she disappeared was her mother's birthday and Moira had convinced her to bake empire biscuits. The girl would not run away the day before her birthday. 'I know my girl,' said Margery Anderson. 'If she was free she would come back home.' They believed someone had abducted their daughter and begged whoever had her to release her unharmed.

'Moira's mother and I are pleading with you to let our little girl go free,' said Andrew Anderson through the pages of the *Daily Record*. 'For five agonising days since Moira's disappearance, we have lived with fear in our hearts. But with faith in God's mercy, we believe Moira will still return alive and well. Have pity on us. We all need her so much.' But if someone had Moira locked away, they ignored the parents' pitiful pleas.

The police did, however, manage to piece together some of the girl's movements after she left her grandmother's house. She had actually been spotted by three people going in the opposite direction from Laird Street and getting on a bus in Alexander Street. She was first seen as she walked through the snow from Muiryhall Street by a woman looking out of her window. As she walked across a piece of waste ground she slipped and fell, picked herself up and continued on her way. Then she was seen by a man who was standing in a tenement doorway opposite the bus stop, sheltering from the snow. This man ran out when his bus came – Baxter's Cliftonville bus going to Old Monkland – but could not say if the girl got on behind him. However, another woman who was already on the bus – and who knew Moira – said the girl did climb on and nodded and smiled at her. However, this witness did not see where the girl got off.

So where was Moira going? And where did she get off? She was also seen by a fourth witness standing at a bus stop in Whifflet, kicking the ground and looking generally as if she was waiting for someone. But who? And did this person pick her up? And if he did, where did he take her?

Her older sister Janet, aged 13, told reporters a story Moira had passed on the night before she disappeared. The story involved a walk down a dark street and a man with a knife. Moira had told Janet about her experience while the two girls walked down Park Street, Coatbridge. 'She pointed to a dark spot and told me that a man had stopped her on Tuesday night as she was taking newspapers to my grandmother,' Janet said, explaining that the man wanted Moira to come with him. 'Moira told me that she started edging away and told the man – who was about 20 – that she didn't want to go. Then she told me the man stepped forward and said "If you don't I'll run a knife into you." Moira told me that by that time she had managed to get a little bit away and she turned and ran.' The police never did trace that young man, while years later, Janet did not even remember telling the story.

Like Janette Hamilton, Mrs Anderson never gave up hope that her daughter was alive. She refused to believe any harm had come to her, taking refuge in her strong religious beliefs. 'I am not giving up hope yet,' she said. 'I feel God is guiding me to Moira.' Sunday 31 March was Mother's Day. It was also Moira's 13th birthday. Her parents had bought her a Monopoly set: she had told them she wanted it the day before she went missing. Mrs Anderson said she would keep it for her until she came home.

The investigation ran its course and Moira was never found. Many of the officers based in the burgh police station in Muiryhall Street, not far from Moira's grandmother's house, worked day and night on the case, scouring the area time and time again for the girl. But the investigation was not without its critics. The most crucial period in any police inquiry is the first 24 hours. Many officers believe that if they do not get a clear break in that period then they will face a long, hard slog before the end is reached, if ever. In this case, according to some, certain steps were not taken. For instance, it would appear that there were no door-to-door inquiries made. (Although later newspaper reports would say that there were.) Official word at the time was that the case had been well publicised and anyone with any information would have come forward. That, however, is a dangerous assumption to make in an investigation such as this. Officers cannot be sure everyone will come forward. Also, the Monklands canal was not dragged. According to the authorities, this could not be done because it was overgrown with weeds. The parents had wanted the burgh police to call in Glasgow CID, who were more experienced in cases of missing children. But this was not done. Police were also urged to have Moira's picture broadcast on BBC television. However, they said the BBC did not transmit the pictures of missing children, and doing so would serve no useful purpose. The BBC said they had not been asked. Following pressure from the local MP, the girl's picture did finally appear on TV at teatime on Saturday 18

May, and although the incident room in Coatbridge received another flood of sightings, all of which proved without foundation, the investigation died.

And the legend began. Someone had heard a car braking to a screeching halt near where the girl had been seen last, so some said she had been knocked down and killed. The driver had then panicked, thrown the body into the boot of his vehicle and taken it away for disposal. But where would they have disposed of the body so efficiently that it has not been found for almost 40 years? Like everywhere else, the Coatbridge area has changed considerably over the years. Old buildings have been demolished while housing schemes have sprouted from what were once open field sites. There were a few such schemes under construction when Moira Anderson disappeared. Her body could have been thrown deep into the foundations of a building, like a block of flats. Or perhaps the killer was not working alone. Her body could have been buried in a garden or under floorboards and someone – a mother, a wife, a father, a brother – could still, 36 years later, be covering up. Perhaps . . .

Part of the legend concerns mass murderer Peter Manuel. Manuel was tried and hanged in 1958 for the murders of the Watt family, the Smart family and Isabel Cooke. He was almost certainly responsible for other murders – including Anne Kneilands in East Kilbride – and there are those who say he also killed Moira. But Manuel was in prison at the time, doing eighteen months for breaking into Hamilton Colliery. He was not released until November 1957. However, this did not prevent detectives from trying to pin the supposed death of Moira Anderson on him. The missing girl was even mentioned during Manuel's trial, when he told the court that detectives had accused him of murdering the girl. But he did not.

During the investigation, the police rounded up all the usual suspects. They interviewed all the local perverts and sexual deviants in the hope that one of them would confess to harming young Moira. One of them was a man called Ian Simpson, who was interviewed no less than three times by

William Muncie, one of Lanarkshire's top detectives. Muncie had an enviable clear-up rate for murder (it has been suggested not always by fair means), but not even he could pin it on Simpson.

In 1962, Simpson thumbed a lift from a Leeds man in the Highlands, shot him dead and buried him in a shallow grave near a lay-by off the A9. He stole the man's car, drove south and picked up a Swiss student making his way home for his sister's wedding. The student's body was found in a Dumfries-shire forest. He, too, had been shot. Simpson was later caught and found unfit to plead and so sent to the state mental hospital at Carstairs. There, in February 1976, he was hacked to death by fellow patients Robert Mone and Thomas McCulloch as they staged a bloody breakout. They also killed a nurse and a police officer during their flight from custody.

In 1963, it was even suggested that Moira Anderson was, in fact, Mandy Rice-Davies. This totally groundless rumour allegedly began when Moira's mother saw the woman's face on television during the publicity surrounding the Profumo scandal.

The case reappeared in magazines and newspapers many times over the years, usually on or near the anniversary of Moira's disappearance. Mrs Anderson died without ever giving up hope that her daughter was alive somewhere. Mr Anderson died, aged 85, on 18 July 1992. A death notice in the local newspaper said that he was the much-loved father of 'Janet, Moira and Marjory'.

Then, a few months after his death, Coatbridge police announced they were re-opening the case. Information had been received, they said. They would not say what and they would not say from whom. But whatever it was, it was convincing enough to warrant a fresh appeal for witnesses, particularly men who were in the town to attend a football match between Airdrieonians and Ayr United – a match cancelled at the last minute because of the severe weather. They also tried to track down the people who saw Moira near the bus stop and on the Old Monkland bus. By 1993, three of them were dead, but the remaining witness remembered the incident well.

Moira's sisters were both married by this time and had moved away from Coatbridge. However, a friend saw the appeals in the newspapers and contacted Marjory, now 43, at her new home in England. She in turn got in touch with 50-year-old Janet, who had emigrated to Australia. Detective Inspector James McEwan, one of the officers in charge of the renewed hunt, was himself holidaying in Australia and his office contacted him with the woman's address. By lucky chance, she was only about 80 miles away from where he was staying and he went down to see her.

Meanwhile the appeal had brought results. Witnesses came forward, including some who had not spoken to the police before. But detectives still had to get out on the streets and track down a number of the original witnesses – including a few of the police officers who had worked the case in 1957. And, more tellingly, on three occasions detectives visited a man in the north of England in connection with the case. However, they have so far refused to comment on whether he was interviewed as a witness or a suspect, emphasising that they are still treating the case as that of a missing person rather than murder. There is still no firm evidence of murder.

'A lot of people came out of the woodwork and gave us a lot of good information regarding the case,' said DI McEwan. 'This was particularly heartening given the passage of time and certainly, some of them don't remember things quite as clearly. But the thing about this case is that it is part of local folklore and everyone who was around at the time remembers where they were when Moira Anderson disappeared. It's a bit like people remembering where you were when Kennedy was shot.' For DI McEwan, his memory was of sliding down a coal bing near Hamilton on a sheet of metal at the age of ten.

But not everyone proved helpful. The police encountered a great deal of resistance from some people who would rather that the matter was allowed to rest. 'It was a surprising wall of silence, I suppose you could call it,' continued DI McEwan.

'Some people just didn't want to know. They didn't want us to rake up the past. Some of them were pretty hostile to us.'

Now transferred from Airdrie CID to Strathclyde Serious Crime Squad, the police officer pledged that the inquiry will continue until every possible avenue has been explored. He remained somewhat tight-lipped about the cause and impetus of the new investigation but made it clear that there is a positive line of inquiry. They are close to a solution, it seems, but not yet close enough. 'But we'll keep going until the circle is complete,' said DI McEwan. 'It's an old cliché really but the Moira Anderson case does prove that cases like this are never really closed.'

However, any future arrest and/or conviction was placed in serious jeopardy by a report in a Sunday newspaper in October 1993 which pointed the finger at the suspect. The article drew the line at actually naming the man but did contain enough information to make it clear who he was, including his age, present location and his occupation at the time of the suspected murder. A good lawyer could possibly make use of this quite extensive publicity to seriously damage the Crown case. Now, even if detectives do manage to make that final connection between this suspect and the disappearance of Moira Anderson, the case, which could rely to a certain extent on identification, may never reach court. The circle may never close . . .

# A Soldier's Story

THE WOMAN SITS in a chair by the fire, a cat curled up by her side, the flames dancing in the grate. She talks softly but lovingly about her son, whose photograph rests on the mantelpiece. It was taken on a holiday and so he is casually dressed, the first shadow of a beard showing. He is looking thoughtfully over his shoulder at something out of frame. As his mother talks, it is impossible not to keep glancing at the man's face, willing it to come to life, to perhaps answer the questions which have haunted his family for three years now. What happened, Sandy? What was worrying you all those months? And who killed you?

Alexander 'Sandy' Drummond was a loving, caring son who stalwartly helped his mother care for her husband who suffers from Alzheimer's disease. He would often pay for holidays to allow her to get away and relax while he stayed at home. He gave much of his money to various charities, at least once giving an entire week's pay to Cancer Research, and regularly gave blood. He loved animals and was often seen building bird boxes.

In his personal life he chose his friends carefully, tending to keep himself to himself, never wishing anyone any harm. He was a gentle man, interested in improving his mind and able to talk on a variety of subjects, with deep and abiding interests in history, astronomy, mathematics and geography. He built by hand a Newtonian telescope, which still lies without its tripod. He took up orienteering and learned Morse code. Weeks before his untimely and tragic death, he sat his City and Guilds, passing with flying colours. He had a strong faith and was shy, but not the loner sometimes painted by the press. 'He had a great tolerance of people's ways,' said Effie

Drummond, his 65-year-old mother. 'He used to say that we're not here to judge what's going on in another person's house. What's their business is theirs. But once he got to know you he was as outgoing as the next person.'

When Sandy was a teenager he wanted to become an engineer and thought the best way to achieve that goal was to join the army and let them teach him the trade. The prospect of the harsh discipline called for in the service did not worry him. 'He was always a well-disciplined boy,' his mother pointed out. 'I never had to chastise him at all.' But he made a mistake in choosing his regiment. At the age of 18, he joined the Black Watch, who rather than teach him engineering put a rifle in his hands and eventually sent him to Northern Ireland. When he realised his mistake he wanted to leave but could not afford to buy himself out so he resolved to serve his three years and then come home.

He spent a total of 18 months in that troubled land across the Irish Sea, where soldiers wonder whether their next step will detonate a booby-trap device or if a sniper's bullet will find them around the next corner. Sandy himself was appalled at the looks of hatred thrown at him by some of the locals. He found these looks difficult to bear and hoped he would never be called on to fire his rifle at anyone. But he survived his tours of duty and left the army to return to his parents' small cottage near Boarhills in Fife, a few miles from St Andrews. This was his home. Here, where the fields roll down neatly to the sea, he should have been safe.

'He spent all that time with the army in Northern Ireland,' says Effie, 'only to be murdered back home by fellow Fifers.'

In the months leading up to what is without a doubt one of the most baffling mysteries in Scotland, Sandy Drummond was a deeply troubled man. His mother would often find him in the greenhouse, sitting with his head in his hands. He would never tell her what was on his mind, probably not wishing to burden her with his troubles.

He had been working at the American-owned Guardbridge paper mill, near Leuchars air base, for eight years. He was a hard worker, keen to do whatever task he was given to the best of his ability. He seldom took his full break period and during the winter had been known to walk through the snow from his home to the mill, pushing his motorcycle. Although he was happy in his work, something apparently had happened shortly after he was transferred to a new department which had forced him to look for another job. 'Whatever it was, I believe he was being persecuted for something,' said Effie. And whatever it was, his employers knew nothing about it.

According to his mother, the trouble seemed to begin during his six years as a web wrapper. To get away from this trouble he changed his job within the mill to that of a labourer, hoping it would be outside work. Unfortunately, though, his mother says this did not seem to work and he appeared to be under greater pressure than ever.

Whatever the cause, Sandy Drummond changed from a cheerful, happy and bouyant personality into a man who seemed to have something permanently on his mind. Whether this mood change had anything to do with Sandy's death has not been established. To be honest, nothing very much has been established.

However, one day it seemed to come to a head and he almost told Effie what was bothering him. 'I was sitting at the fire here one day and Sandy was sitting opposite me, his back to me. I was day dreaming, one of the cats on my knee, when I was aware of his back jerking slightly. I knew right away that he was crying and I couldn't believe it – it was something I'd never seen him do in his life, even when he was a bairn. He could withstand a lot of pain, you see. He'd had two big spinal operations and he never moaned, not once.' Knowing there was something not quite right, Effie Drummond asked him what was wrong. Her son shook his head. 'Sandy,' she said, 'please tell me what's wrong?'

Sandy turned then, tears welling in his eyes, again shaking his head. 'I can't, mum,' he said. 'it's too filthy to repeat to my mother.'

Within weeks, he was dead.

The body was found at about eight p.m. on Monday, 24 June 1991 on a farm track yards away from the cottage Sandy had been sharing with his brother, Jimmy, since January 1990. He was lying face down in the grass, his arms under his trunk, legs out straight. Both the doctor and the first police officer on the scene thought the position was unusual for someone who may have collapsed. The doctor examining the body at the locus found superficial abrasions on the elbows and forehead and commented that it had all the hallmarks of a suspicious death. And that was how Sandy Drummond's death was described for the next eight months. It certainly was suspicious. It was also murder.

The post-mortem was carried out by Professor Derrick Pounder of Dundee Royal Infirmary. The body was referred to him with no suggestion of any suspicious circumstances and on examination, he found additional bruises on the back and neck. In his opinion, the mechanism of death was asphyxiation and obstruction of the flow of blood to the brain, probably caused by a third party. Three days afterwards, Effie Drummond phoned him and he told her that her son had, in his opinion, been strangled. 'I couldn't believe it,' Effie recalled. 'I thought, no – not my Sandy.'

But the police still had not announced that the man had been murdered. A detective inspector would later say that there had been a possibility in his mind that death had been caused by natural causes and there had been 'a common conclusion' that Sandy Drummond could have been clutching his stomach when he fell. That could explain why the locus was not treated as a murder scene – had not been taped off, the body and surrounding area protected – so any forensic clues which may have been present were lost.

In fact, it would be a further eight months before the police publicly announced that the case was one of murder. They have not explained exactly why they kept full details of the murder investigation quiet, saying it was a Crown Office decision. That decision could be viewed as a serious error. As we now know, the first 24 to 48 hours in any inquiry are the most important. If it was known that Sandy Drummond's mysterious death was murder soon after the discovery of the body, then the media should have been used to appeal to potential witnesses. Certainly, there were small stories, for instance in the *Glasgow Herald*, labelling the case as a suspicious death. Had it been known the case was one of murder, then it could be argued that the stories would have received greater prominence, thus attracting more reader attention. The area is a favourite for tourists and day trippers and at that time of year an untold number of cars could have been driving along that particular road to and from St Andrews. Some of these motorists could have seen something important without realising it – and not knowing that the man had been murdered may not have thought to come forward. After eight months, when the investigation was confirmed as a homicide and fuller details released, their memories could have dimmed. Someone with a vital piece of information may not have come forward because that most important word – murder – was not used.

The details concerning the strange events in the days before Sandy's death were first made public in BBC TV's *Crimewatch UK* in February 1992. Mrs Drummond, her eldest son, Jimmy, and other witnesses assisted in the making of the film, an actor playing Sandy. According to the police, the Crown Office gave their permission to release full details of the case for the first time while Mrs Drummond told officers that she would not co-operate in the making of the film unless it was publicly proclaimed that her son was in fact murdered. 'I had been saying it to the media all the time,' she said. 'If I knew it from day three then so should they.'

Sandy Drummond made some most uncharacteristic moves in those final few days. First, he had, without warning, handed in his notice at the mill. Effie Drummond says that on Thursday 20 June, he was apparently working as normal and sent to carry out a job in another part of the mill. Within 30 or 45 minutes he was in the administration office, telling them he could not work at the mill anymore and he walked out, never to return. The police, however, say that he did not announce his intention to leave until the Friday morning,

when he phoned in to say he would not be back. They con-
cede though that he certainly made that decision on the
Thursday as he had left keys which he would have needed the
following day. No one knows what it was that made him take
such a decisive step, but he meant what he said.

This sudden decision took his employers by surprise as he
had always been such a keen worker. When he was told that
he would have to give a week's notice, he said in a letter that
would not be beneficial to either the company or himself.
What he meant by that is a mystery. 'It wasn't like Sandy,' said
his mother. 'I know he had been looking for another job but
he was never one to leave without having something else lined
up. He had never been on the dole.'

He did not tell his mother what he had done. He had
Sunday dinner with her and his father as usual and she noted
that for some reason he was like the old Sandy again,
whistling happily as he performed odd jobs around the house.
As he left that night, he gave his mother her customary cuddle
and rode off on his motorbike. At the top of the lane leading
to the cottage he waved and turned right towards St Andrews,
the opposite direction from his cottage near Boarhills. That
was the last time she saw him alive.

When this scene was being re-enacted for the *Crimewatch*
cameras, Effie Drummond said that just for a moment, the
actor playing her son looked so much like him. She stepped
forward and he seemed to know what she was about to ask
and opened his arms to let her hug him. 'I knew it wasn't
really Sandy,' she recalled, 'but somehow it was if I was able
to say goodbye to him through this man.'

But leaving his job so suddenly was not the only out-of-
character move made by the usually dependable Sandy
Drummond in those last mystifying days. He had withdrawn
£850 – practically all his savings – from his accounts with the
Bank of Scotland and the Dunfermline Building Society.
(Most of this money was later found in his home, so robbery
was not the motive for murder.) He had told his brother the
night before he died that he had 'jacked in' his job on
Thursday and planned to take off on his bike and travel

around a bit, probably staying in the tent. His brother had offered him the use of the car, which Sandy first accepted, then, on the Monday morning, decided against it. The last time Jimmy spoke to Sandy was that morning as he left to go to work himself.

The full events of that last day remain unknown. At 7.25 a.m. a motorist passing by Falside Cottage in his car saw someone run out of the front door with a bag under his arms and dart across the road, vaulting a hedge into the field opposite. Yet when the driver drew level with the point where he had seen the figure last, the man was nowhere in sight. The sports bag he carried has never been found. Who was this person? The motorist thought it might have been Sandy but Effie Drummond says her son would never have used the front door and would have no reason to hide on the other side of the road. 'Anyway,' she continued, 'Sandy was seen on his motorbike at that time, heading to St Andrews. He was positively identified by two witnesses.'

Whoever that was running out of the cottage, Sandy was definitely in St Andrews later that morning. The video cameras of the Dunfermline Building Society in St Andrews recorded him coming in at 11 a.m. to withdraw his money. Meanwhile, a man wearing similar clothes – a sleeveless denim jacket, yellow t-shirt, army camouflage-type trousers and black boots – and with a similar build to Sandy – five foot seven inches tall, of slim to medium build and with short brown balding hair – was spotted jogging along the road at about four p.m. Three-quarters of an hour later a rusty orange car, possibly an old Morris Marina, was seen parked outside the cottage and two men seen through the living-room window.

Sandy – or someone like him – may have been seen again in Boarhills at around seven p.m., while at 7.15 p.m. a red hatchback car was seen reversing at the bottom of the farm track where the dead man was found 45 minutes later. Again at around 7.15 p.m. two men leaped out of a silver Renault 5 or Volkswagen at the bridge very near to where Sandy was found, jumped over a wall, dropping about nine feet to a grassy field and running in the direction of the farm track, up a small hill and through some trees and bushes.

Police had also appealed for information from a young woman seen walking her dog up the track at about one o'clock that afternoon, as well as tourists visiting the area and anglers fishing in the nearby Kelty Burn. The *Crimewatch* programme prompted about 30 calls to the special hotline number. But none of them brought police any nearer to solving the case.

Every employee at the mill was questioned during the investigation. They even looked into Sandy's army record, travelling the length and breadth of the country to interview squaddies with whom Sandy had served. No one had a bad word to say about the dead man, there was not a breath of scandal, prompting one detective to comment that this guy was cleaner than the Archangel Gabriel. No one, it seemed, wished him ill.

But someone obviously did. At some time during that final day, Sandy met that person – or persons – and he was murdered. Why, and even where and when, remains a mystery. Had he stumbled on something that he shouldn't? What possible reason could anyone have for killing this man who seemingly did not have an enemy in the world? The police believe that if they had managed to trace the orange car seen at the cottage they may have found their murderer. But the car, they feel, was probably disposed of very quickly.

Following pressure from the Drummond family, the Lord Advocate ordered a fatal accident inquiry, after the 15-month-long police investigation had failed to track down the killer. It was unusual for the Crown Office to take such a step in a case like this but Effie Drummond was not to be refused. The proceedings were held during September 1992 by Sheriff Charles Smith.

During the three-day inquiry, the Sheriff heard from Effie Drummond how Sandy was a quiet country lad whose life had been made a 'hell on earth' by certain people at work. His brother said that on the night before he died, Sandy had written the men's names down and had tried to contact them.

Then came the evidence of a second pathologist, who had some strong words to say concerning the initial investigation into the cause of death. He said that there had been inadequate examination of the body at the scene and a doctor experienced in dealing with murder would have spotted tiny haemorrhages in the dead man's eyes. These spots, known as petechiae or Tardieu spots after the French surgeon who first described them, appear when increased blood pressure causes small capillaries in the eye to rupture during suffocation or strangling. Had these signs been noted at an early stage, the information could have been passed on to the police. The body should have been left where it was found and proper precautions taken to safeguard potential evidence.

Professor Anthony Busuttil of Edinburgh University had been asked by the Crown Office to give a second opinion on the case. His early findings, he said, indicated homicide. In fact, he felt that Sandy could have been killed somewhere else, his body bundled into a car or other vehicle and then merely dumped on the farm track. The professor said he could not totally exclude the possibility that the murder had occurred at the track but he had, he said, 'used the pieces of a jigsaw to produce a picture'. He said: 'Death appears to have been sudden and the deceased not having put up any major struggle suggests he was either taken unawares or the death was not premeditated in any way.' However, due to what he called the 'inadequate examination of the body where it was found' there was little he could go on regarding the time of death. He admitted that his words were strongly critical. 'If one finds a body in an unusual situation and it shows no external features of natural disease, I believe that the death in every single instance has to be looked at fully,' he said, 'and by that I mean the presence of a doctor with experience in looking at these deaths at the locus.' Had the tell-tale Tardieu spots been noted at an early stage, it would have been known that this was not a natural death.

On the final day of the inquiry, Sheriff Charles Smith blocked attempts by the Drummond family solicitor to pose questions regarding the four-month delay between the death and the launching of an official murder investigation. The solicitor, Richard McFarlane, said that the police had treated the case as a suspicious death until October 1991, despite the report from Professor Pounder that it was probably a homicide. Mr McFarlane asked: 'One question Mrs Drummond wants to know the answer to is why, if police were aware they were dealing with a homicide as of six p.m. on 25 June, it took approximately 117 days for police to acknowledge that fact to her?'

Sheriff Smith said he did not wish to go further in this inquiry than the time of death, that his remit did not cover questions regarding the police investigation. 'This is not an inquiry into the police investigation,' he said, 'and I am not prepared to allow that line of questioning.'

But Mr McFarlane was not going to let it rest, asking: 'How can we find out the circumstances of the death if there aren't procedures to safeguard evidence?' The solicitor pointed out that this was 'a unique inquiry'. They had an unlawful killing and someone – or some people – were responsible for bringing Sandy Drummond's life to an end. An airing of the police investigation could be beneficial, he thought.

But Sheriff Smith dug in his judicial heels, saying: 'What you are seeking to inquire is how evidence was obtained and if it was obtained efficiently and that I am not prepared to listen to.'

The Sheriff said he had enough information on which to base his ruling that Sandy Drummond died by strangulation and that the death was homicidal. He said that earlier criticism of witnesses had been made with the qualification that, with hindsight, everyone had perfect vision. He also felt that, at the end of the day, the FAI might trigger the memories of witnesses and possibly lead to new lines of inquiry. But there have been no new lines of inquiry. The police investigation is still live but lying dormant, waiting for further information to come in. Little, if any, has come in. The killer, or killers, remain free.

Effie Drummond, meanwhile, has vowed never to give up. She wants the truth to come out and the guilty parties to receive the justice they deserve. 'Sandy lived by the New Testament,' she said, 'and turned the other cheek. I cannot do that. The people who did this are monsters, scum. I call them the Devil's spawn. They can take my son away from me but they cannot take away my faith, my memories or my anger.'

She is bitter over the lack of progress in the investigation, especially in the early days. She said: 'With the help of honest people there will be a day of reckoning. The truth cannot be twisted. The FAI proved my great misgiving and I shall not rest until true justice is done.' She believes there were blunders made and she has had to do things, to learn things, that should not be expected of any ordinary person. 'May God give me the strength and help I need to sort out this unforgivable foul up,' she said.

However, she said that a lot of people, including some police officers, MPs and lawyers, have been very kind to her. But she believes that someone is covering up for the culprit and wishes that person would come forward and ease her torment. She has put up all her life savings as a reward for information which leads to a conviction. She also talks regularly with journalists interested in the case and has appeared on television to discuss it.

Meanwhile, the killers are aware of her stand and may be attempting to frighten her into silence. She says a strange car has been seen parked in the shadows of the lane near her home, while there have been curious noises outside at night. Newspapers left on her doorstep have been slashed and, more recently, a wrought-iron side gate was pulled off its hinges and an ornamental fringe snapped off. She also insists her house was broken into on one occasion last September. Nothing was taken, but there were signs that the front door had been tampered with, a side window was lying open and her back door, which was locked and chained before she left to go to St Andrews that morning, was unlocked. A large dark handprint found on the inside of the door was dismissed by police as 'unimportant'.

And while she continues her fight for justice, she sees signs of her dead son everywhere. Sandy Drummond was a keen horticulturist and would order seeds for wild plants and flowers and travel the length and breadth of Fife on his motorbike, planting them in fields and on roadsides, for others to appreciate, to keep them alive for future generations. Now whenever Effie passes by a spot graced by a riot of colour where before there had been none, she knows her son has been there ahead of her. It's not much, but at least it's something.

# The Dogs of War

THE STOCKY FIGURE walking alone on the Glasgow street may not have known what was happening at first. He may have heard the sounds – just a series of loud cracks – but we will never know. Perhaps there was a grazing pain at his cheek as one bullet spun harmlessly past. There would have been a sharper agony searing across his back as another bullet fractured two ribs. Then, as he doubled over in pain, a third punched into his left-hand side below his ribs, boring into his abdominal cavity, piercing a kidney before continuing through his stomach and liver and finally careering through his heart.

But he did not fall. The man stumbled forward as the bullets ploughed into him but did not lose his footing, remaining on his feet as he saw his sister come rushing out from her house. 'I've been shot, hen,' he managed to say, his arms stretching out to her. 'I'm going to collapse . . .' And then he slid to the pavement, landing on his knees, still very little blood showing from the wounds.

He was still alive when his family hefted him into a car and drove at breakneck speed through the city streets to Glasgow's Royal Infirmary. He was still alive when he arrived at the accident and emergency unit, where the surgical team tried to revive him. He had been shot at precisely 11.09 p.m. on Saturday, 17 August 1991. Within an hour he was dead.

He was not the only man to die violently in the second city that night. A short time before the gun spat death from the darkness in Provanmill, a young soldier on leave from his regiment found himself involved in a fight outside a pub in Barlanark, in the East End. Gunner Robert Mills had come through what crime writer Ed McBain has called 'that mini-series in the Gulf' with barely a scratch but in the confusion

143

of the fight outside the Caravel bar, someone plunged a knife into him, leaving him for dead on the pavement. Eventually, a man was tried for the killing but was acquitted.

But the murder of that young father did not catch the imagination of the city. It did not spark off a huge and costly manhunt or lead to the murders of another two men or finally to Scotland's longest-running murder trial. It was the death of the stocky man in Provanmill Road which did all that. It also laid bare the workings of Glasgow's underworld, a strata of society which normally prefers to operate outwith public scrutiny, revealing it to be a violent world of guns and grenades, of drugs and death, of kneecappings and knifings. City politicians, who spent so much time – not to mention money – on changing the razor-slashing image of Glasgow were rending their civic gowns publicly as they saw much of their work being swept away in a flood of blood and destruction. The so-called underworld was a culture whose existence they preferred not to acknowledge. But the trial and resultant media coverage would show that there is indeed a cancer behind the city's smart new sand-blasted façade; perhaps not terminal but certainly inoperable. However, at the end of it all, all four slayings – including the tragic death of Gunner Mills – would remain unsolved.

The man shot to death that night was Arthur Thompson Jnr, known to some as the Godfather's son, to others less respectfully as 'the Mars Bar Kid'. In his death he achieved a fame which some insiders say he was unlikely to achieve in life.

His father, though, was something else again. For 30 years, Arthur Thompson's name was legend in Glasgow. They said he was the top gangster in the city, a friend of the Kray twins and that there was not a criminal pie in the East End – if not the entire city – in which he had not inserted a finger. Or two. And there were a few fingers which he had, figuratively speaking, cut off over the years. And perhaps not even figuratively speaking.

But despite it being common knowledge that the man they called Big Arthur was Glasgow's criminal overlord, the police could not lay a glove on him. He was untouchable, unassailable and unshakable in his own assertions that he was only a businessman. Even rival hoodlums found he led a charmed life when he survived three murder attempts, one of which claimed the life of his mother-in-law in a car-bomb attack in 1966.

He once said: 'I am the first to admit that, in 20 or 30 years, I've picked up a reputation. I've been charged and accused of a lot of things, including culpable homicide and robbery. But I've only been to prison once in the past 20 years . . .'

This was true. He was jailed in 1968 for four years for his part in a warehouse burglary which netted £3,000. It was Big Arthur's last taste of porridge. His first conviction came in 1949 when, at the age of 18, he was fined for an assault. Sentences for robbery, extortion and reset (receiving stolen goods) followed. He received two years for a bank job with safeblower Paddy Meehan – they blew the safe of the Beauly bank while the local law slept a short distance away down the street.

During the following decade and a half he rose in Glasgow's criminal hierarchy and in notoriety within the city in general. He befriended the Kray twins in London, allegedly sending some of his hardest men to 'the Smoke' to act as enforcers. It was said that even the toughest London hood walked in fear of these wild men from the north.

Back home in Glasgow, east enders on the fringes of gangsterdom liked to claim links with Big Arthur. As they sipped pints in dingy bars on Duke Street and London Road they recounted tales of his violence and brutality with a relish and even an admiration that outsiders claim is unique to Glasgow. But it is not: scratch the surface of any city and you will find men like Arthur Thompson; scratch further and you will uncover the ordinary citizens who lionise them.

By the mid-Sixties Thompson was big enough to have dangerous enemies. He found himself embroiled in a feud with a family named Welsh, while in 1966 his mother-in-law perished in the car-bomb attack meant for him. Thompson had driven his car only yards from his front door when the device went off, throwing him clear but leaving him badly injured. Three members of the Welsh family were accused of the murder but found not guilty. Thompson himself gave evidence against them, making legal history that day for appearing in the same court twice, once as a witness and once as an accused: one hour before the three Welsh brothers climbed into the dock, Thompson himself had stood there, accused of murdering James Welsh and Arthur Goldie by forcing their van off the road and into a wall with his Jaguar. He too was found not guilty by the jury. It was all grist to the mill for the Thompson storytellers. Big Arthur was too big for them to touch, they said. They wouldn't get him. But they did – two years later he received his sentence for the warehouse robbery.

When he got out, he became more circumspect in his dealings, placing buffers between himself and his criminal dealings. His interests expanded. He formed silent partnerships with legitimate pub owners. They say some of them did not have a choice in the matter. And while running legitimate businesses like pubs, dance-halls, gaming clubs, betting shops, scrap-metal dealerships, car salerooms and even a timber outlet, he was also allegedly into such nice little criminal earners as money-lending, extortion and bankrolling armed robberies. Rumours abounded of his involvement in these lucrative criminal enterprises but no one managed to prove it. Or no one wanted to.

But although prison had been written out of his future, there was always a young gun out to make his name. In 1988 he was shot by a man who just wanted to be the man who shot Arthur Thompson. The gangster was rushed in a friend's Rolls-Royce to a private clinic where he received treatment – saying he had been injured by a flying drill bit during home improvements. The young gunman was never convicted, not for the shooting anyway.

And so, the legend of Arthur Thompson continued to grow. But as the Eighties progressed he began to scale down his business interests. He was getting older now. He still had a joinery business and he received £94 a week invalidity benefit following the 1988 shooting. His house in Provanmill Road was a monument to the ranch-house style so beloved of the Glasgow gangster. He had a villa in Spain but seldom went there because, at least according to reporters, his wife did not like to miss *Coronation Street*. He was, they said, a multi-millionaire but none of his cash was kept in Britain. He could afford to slow down, perhaps even retire. He even had time to help in the campaign to have his old friend Paddy Meehan pardoned for a murder he did not commit. His criminal empire would pass into the hands of his son.

However, young Arthur, Fat Boy, was no chip off the old block. He was not even a shaving. He was, according to many who knew him, loud-mouthed and boastful, lacking the intelligence and even sophistication of his father. When Big Arthur reputedly hesitated about involving himself in the rapidly expanding drugs trade, it was his son who embraced it. The anecdote mirrors the fictional scenes in Mario Puzo's *The Godfather*, in which the ageing Don refuses to becoming part of the narcotics business, against the wishes of his hot-headed and loud-mouthed son, Santino. Like young Arthur, Santino died in a hail of bullets.

According to the stories, it was young Arthur who recognised the money to be made from the smokin', shootin' and snortin' crowd. The city's drugs trade really only took off in the late Seventies and early Eighties, until in 1992 it was estimated that it was worth something in the region of £180 million. With such a burgeoning market just waiting out there for some bright entrepreneur to take control it was only a matter of time before the big boys moved in. The customers were there, ready and willing to take as much 'hash', 'blaw' (cannabis), 'sulph' (amphetamine), 'coke' (cocaine) and 'smack' (heroin) as they could supply. Then there were those understudies for heroin like 'tems' (the painkiller Temgesic) and 'eggs' (Temazepam tranquillisers) as well as LSD, the icon of the Sixties when it was fashionable to turn on, tune in and drop out, and such recent developments as 'Eccies' (Ecstasy, otherwise known as Methylenedioxymethylamphetamine, or MDMA for short).

Of course, there was violence. Glasgow was no stranger to the law of the blade and gun and occasionally someone would get out of line or try to move into someone else's territory and have to be given 'a message'. Usually, this message amounted to a quick slashing or a kneecapping but now and again, the message boys would go too far and the police would be investigating a murder. Often, their investigations would be met with a sullen silence with potential witnesses being suddenly stricken with three-wise-monkey fever – they saw nothing, heard nothing and were saying nothing.

Meanwhile, the Thompsons' drug interests took on an ironic tinge in June 1989 when Arthur's daughter, Margaret, choked on her own vomit following an overdose of drugs and alcohol.

Generally, though, the suppliers – the wholesalers – were untouched by the trade. By the time their merchandise reached the streets it had passed through so many hands and travelled in so many directions that it was practically impossible to trace it back to them. The police made arrests, of course, but they were generally the users and the dealers, the bottom-most rungs in the drugs ladder.

But in 1985, the law caught up with Arthur Thompson Jnr and he was sentenced to 11 years for possession of heroin with intent to supply. His trial, at the High Court in Glasgow, was peppered with allegations that he was the victim of a 'fit-up' by officers of Strathclyde Police's drugs squad and serious crime squad. On his conviction, the trial judge said that the verdict of the jury 'completely exonerated the officers of these squads of the allegations made against them'. Yet, throughout his term in prison Thompson continued to protest his innocence, once even tearing up papers for early release because he said it would mean admitting his guilt.

However, it was apparently common knowledge that young Arthur, the man who would be king, was still conducting his drugs business from inside prison, using the access to public pay-phones now allowed to most prisoners to make coded deals with his contacts outside. But this is said about most big-time drug dealers once they are caught – and if it was so well known why could the authorities not catch him at it and put a stop to it? The police are not averse to tapping phones – legally or illegally it seems – when the need arises. Also, the pay-phones in prisons are allegedly monitored as a matter of course. Or were the man's verbal codes just too complex to crack? And if it was such common knowledge, should the man not have been under surveillance during his prison leave? And if that was the case, where were his police watchers at the time of his death?

Whatever the case, young Thompson had angered somebody. Even while he was inside, other prisoners were telling journalists that he was a 'marked man who would not survive long outside'. While he was in prison, a rival mob was making inroads into the drugs scene and muscling in on his operation. Known as the Barlanark Team, after the East End scheme from which they sprang, the gang had formed in the Seventies and specialised in armed raids and robberies of post offices and warehouses. Some of them had moved into drug dealing in the early Eighties and with young Arthur out of the way saw the chance to make a bid to take over the business right across the city.

While young Arthur was doing his time, associates on the outside were waging war on the Barlanark Team. The Caravel bar – the alleged haunt of some of the Barlanark boys and the same pub where Robert Mills died – was torched in 1988. Later, a live grenade – in actual fact a NATO-issue fragmentation device – was rolled under a car at the front door of the pub, where it was spotted and first dumped in a nearby cemetery before being moved to a disused railway line. The police were then called and the army arrived to blow the device up. Rival crooks shot, stabbed, crippled and maimed each other. One was blinded, his one good eye skewered on the edge of a blade.

According to some reports, Thompson Jnr also felt forced to 'grass' on some of them to bring them to heel. His family denied that this was the case but if it was true then naturally, these gentlemen would be somewhat peeved. The alleged 'grass' would be a sudden death waiting for a locus.

According to some sources, Big Arthur had to hire prison 'minders' to protect his boy from ill-wishers on the inside.

Meanwhile, young Arthur seemed to have plans of his own. It was revealed that just before his death young Arthur had been in a pub boasting that he had drawn up a hit list of rival gangsters who, he claimed, had crossed him at some point or another. Two of them would later be found execut-ed gangland-style in a car parked in an East End side street. Not only that, but he was also said to be plotting to murder a high-ranking detective with a car bomb, partly as revenge for having him arrested, partly to warn other officers away from future investigations. But someone got to young Arthur first.

The 'hit' was no spur-of-the-moment decision, it was care-fully planned and executed. Arthur Thompson Jnr was on his first weekend leave from Noranside open prison, near Forfar in Angus, when he was gunned down. Inmates at this prison are eligible for such 'training-for-freedom' leave six weeks after they are transferred there – and the killers knew that. It was Saturday, 17 August 1991 and the 31-year-old gang boss had gone to an Indian restaurant near the city's Charing Cross for a meal earlier with his common-law wife, Catherine, his sister and her boyfriend. While they were there someone walked into the restaurant and asked about them. That man was never traced.

After the meal, they returned to the family home at Provanmill Road – the Thompson family occupied two end terraces within yards of each other, both converted and refur-bished in the ranch-house style that gave them the nicknames 'the Ponderosa' and 'South Fork', depending on which televi-sion show the user favoured. At just after 11, he decided to walk the short distance from his father's home at number 176 Provanmill Road to his own at number 186. He never made it.

The assassin fired six bullets from behind a parked car. Three hit their mark but only one proved fatal. His sister, Tracy, had walked her brother to the door and heard the sounds. 'I thought it was a car backfiring,' she would later say in court, 'and then I realised it was a gun going off.' She said that there were no marks on young Arthur when she saw him, no blood. She asked: 'What's happened?' 'I've been shot, hen,' he gasped. 'I'm going to collapse.'

Tracy Thompson grabbed her brother and he went down on to his knees. The 26-year-old woman then ran back into her parents' house, shouting that Arthur had been shot. Her mother and father ran into the street while she telephoned for an ambulance. No one phoned the police because, unsurprisingly, no one trusted them. By the time Tracy Thompson got back into the street, her niece, Amanda – the dying man's daughter – was lying on top of her father, trying to bring him round. His wife was bringing the car to the scene, ready to rush the wounded man to hospital. He died at 18 minutes past midnight.

The tabloid press had a field day. Monday's headlines screamed sensationally about the killing – DRUG GANG WAR FEARS, £50,000 HIT-MAN MURDERS HOOD – because there is nothing the tabloids and the reading public like better than a juicy crimeland thriller. And this one, from their point of view, would just get better and better. The Scottish *Sun* said that top gangland figures not only in Glasgow but also in Liverpool and Newcastle all had grudges against Thompson Jnr and that the man had received an untold number of death threats while in prison, hence the prison minders. The reports quoted an anonymous underworld source – such sources are always anonymous, no matter what newspaper they talk to – who said that these 'wealthy people' were 'prepared to throw in 50 grand to get him'. But the 'hit' could be put down to at least ten different people, it seems. The source closed by saying that young Arthur 'lived by the sword and died by the sword'. As an epitaph it made up in accuracy what it lacked in originality.

A police officer was quoted as saying, perhaps naïvely: 'Without knowing the motive behind (the attack) we can't speculate on whether any of the other members of the family are at risk.' But later, a senior detective would say that he had previously warned Big Arthur, his son and other gangsters that their lives were in danger. The senior Thompson's characteristically laconic view was that 'he must've had a crystal ball'. Speaking a few days after the murder, the older man said that he had no idea who did it or for what reason. 'Maybe it was a case of mistaken identity,' he said, disingenuously. 'Or maybe someone had it in for me.'

Certainly, he had survived yet another dramatic attempt on his life in May 1990 when a white Escort XR3i rammed into him, propelled him through a fence and then proceeded to try and reverse over him. According to witnesses, Thompson pulled out a gun and fired at the car, which drove off. One man went over to help him up but a young man wearing dark glasses also turned up and assisted his boss home. The would-be Good Samaritan said he did not see a gun being used.

But when the police, alerted by residents, followed a trail of blood to Arthur Thompson's door, he refused to tell them anything. Later he would admit to being the victim of a minor hit-and-run after he had walked home from a nearby pub somewhat the worse for drink and singing his heart out. 'Someone obviously didn't like my singing,' he claimed with his typical flair for understatement, not to mention misdirection.

Some time after the 'accident', a 9mm Beretta was found by police on wasteground near the scene following that ever-faithful means of communication, the anonymous tip-off. The police would describe the pistol some time later as a collector's piece manufactured in 1923. When discovered, it was cocked with one bullet in the breech and another three in the magazine. It was unsafe and had it been thrown a considerable distance would almost certainly have gone off. Old Arthur said he had never seen it before and wouldn't even know how to load it. The incident was forgotten by the press and public but would return to the headlines again during the murder trial.

Soon, detectives were linking a brutal kneecapping committed on 26 May 1991 to the slaying. A man said he accepted a lift from two mysterious strangers on the A77 Glasgow to Ayr road near to Malletsheugh near Newton Mearns. He told the police that he was taken to a lay-by near the Eaglesham cut-off and told to get out of the car. He was then shot in the legs with a handgun. Following the murder of Arthur Thompson Jnr, the victim – William Gillen – claimed that the gunmen were hired to get him after an argument with a convicted killer during a jail visit.

But ballistic evidence would prove that the same gun was used in both the kneecapping and the Arthur Thompson Jnr murder. The gun itself has never been recovered, although two men would later be arrested and charged with the Gillen shooting. But only one of them would make it to trial.

The pub worker had seen the car, a blue Orion, sitting in Darlieth Street near his place of employment when he arrived for work at nine o'clock on the morning of Wednesday, 18 September 1991. He hadn't really thought much about it at the time. Then, at about half past ten that morning, a man came into the pub, the Cottage bar on Shettleston Road, saying he thought there was someone lying in the front seat of the car. The pub employee and the customer went out to investigate . . . and found two bodies, one slumped on the floor in the front, the other in the back. It seemed to be a typical gangland-style execution, the victims told to kneel down with their hands over their eyes and then killed quickly with a bullet to the back of the head. The pistol was used at such close range that powder burns were found on the bodies.

The pub worker recognised the men as his boss Robert Glover and Joe 'Bananas' Hanlon. Glover owned the Cottage bar and had also appeared in Kilmarnock sheriff court charged with the shooting of William Gillen in May. But he had been released on bail – unlike his alleged accomplice, who was remanded to Barlinnie prison to await trial. But more of him later. Both murdered men, it was said, were members of the Barlanark Team: Hanlon as an enforcer; Glover in an unspecified role, although his pub was supposed to have been used on occasion as an unofficial headquarters for the gang.

The police and their attendant experts descended on the

area, taping off the street from gawping onlookers and press-men eager for pictures. Fingerprint men dusted, photogra-phers focused, video cameras filmed. Officers spoke to local residents who told them that the car had not been parked there the previous night and no one had seen or heard any-thing untoward, suggesting that the murders had been com-mitted elsewhere and the car merely driven to the street beside the bar and left there, perhaps as a warning to those involved.

Shortly after the investigating team arrived, Mr Paul Hanlon, the brother of one of the murdered men, also arrived, asking what the commotion was in Darlieth Street. He was told by police officers that his brother had been found dead in the car. The man tried to force his way past the police cor-don to reach the car but was held back and led away by a CID officer. Although he came back later, the man was again taken away by the police, this time in the back of a police car. Onlookers could see he was sobbing.

Three hours after the discovery of the deaths, the car was loaded on to a police recovery vehicle – with the corpses still inside but covered by blankets – and taken away to allow forensic scientists to inspect the vehicle away from the media glare and pathologists to conduct their own grisly duties in private.

Meanwhile, as the lorry bearing the car pulled away from the murder scene, mourners were gathering in Riddrie ceme-tery for the funeral of Arthur Thompson Jnr. Among them were politicians and personalities, rubbing expensively suited shoulders with a host of anonymous hard-faced men sporting elaborate jewellery and 'chib' marks, Glasgow's equivalent of duelling scars. The flowers around the grave would not have looked out of place on the set of a Hollywood gangster epic.

Meanwhile, detectives were being cautious in their state-ments to the press, downplaying any suggestion of a link between the Thompson killing and the new double murder. 'There's no indication of a connection,' said Detective Chief Superintendent Pat Connor, joint head of the Strathclyde's CID, 'but it's something we may have to consider.'

But reporters and the public had already considered that

possibility and decided the deaths were indeed in some way connected. Satisfied members of the Arthur Thompson Appreciation Society nodded sagely as they sipped their pints, considering the dramatic edge of the double 'hit'. The Big Man was back, they said to anyone who would listen. He was still In Charge. Two of theirs for one of his – and on the day of his boy's funeral. That's stylish that, so it is.

So, with the existence of a murderous gang war raging in the city streets now public knowledge, the police decided it was time for some high-profile action. A joint incident room was set up in the city's London Road police station to investigate the three murders. They announced that they were to increase their presence in the East End and north-west of the city – news which would be far from music to the ears of many small-time crooks. Over the following months, the police would claim that this increased presence – involving not only increased beat patrols but also the deployment of unmarked vans filled with plainclothes officers and known as Operation Spur – would hoover up a number of car thieves, housebreakers and assorted troublemakers unconnected to the gang war.

The blue H-registered Orion was owned by Joe Hanlon, who received his nickname 'Bananas' either through a wild, some say violent, act after which a friend said 'He's bananas, that guy' or following his dressing up as a banana during a charity event. Like his co-victim, Robert Glover, he had also been charged several weeks before with a violent crime, this time of attempted murder and serious assault in which another gangland figure was blinded after being stabbed in the eye. Like his friend Robert Glover, Joseph Hanlon was bailed on what was a very serious charge. And like the assault on William Gillen, that charge would loom large in the Arthur Thompson murder trial.

Both men had been named to the police as possible suspects in the Arthur Thompson slaying. In fact, Glover's car had been impounded by police looking for evidence in both the killing and the Gillen shooting. But Glover fervently denied being involved in either incident, telling the Scottish

*Sun*'s crime reporter, Stephen Wilkie, just days before he was murdered: 'The police seem to think I am connected with the Thompson shooting and are determined to make the Gillen charges stick. If they do come up with something then it will have to be a fabrication.' He went on to say that he was confident police would find no evidence in his car because his son ate chocolate in it regularly, often leaving it so dirty it had to be valeted every weekend. 'So I know there's nothing in the motor to connect it with that incident,' he continued. He told the reporter that he had heard his name was being 'fired in' for the Thompson murder and had received a threatening phone call pointing out 'his card was marked'. 'There's no way I want to be killed in revenge for a shooting that's not down to me,' he said.

It has to be said that this is a common ploy adopted by Glasgow criminals. Throw a brick into Glasgow's Barlinnie prison and you will hit 100 men who claim they were fitted up by the police for their crimes. Throw another one and you'll hit a few who may even have written to the chief constable – or had their lawyer write – some time before their arrest, pointing out their fears. Strangely enough, young Arthur had his solicitor do just that months before his arrest on the drug charges which would have him convicted for 11 years.

(This does not mean though that Glover was involved in the Gillen shooting or the Thompson murder. Nor does it mean that some police officers do not on occasion 'fit up' criminals. Unhappily, it is more common than the public choose to believe. Some officers claim, privately of course, that it is the only way they have of seeing their quarry put away. If they do not manufacture evidence and/or lie in court then the big villains would escape justice, aided by a system which is weighted heavily in their favour – which it is not, despite publicity to the contrary – while 'clever' lawyers twist the police officer's own words against them. And 'clever' in cop-speak can often mean 'crooked'. Sir David McNee, a former head of Glasgow Police and later Commissioner of the Metropolitan Police, once described this practice as 'pious perjury'. It is tempting to justify such actions by saying that the police are doing it for society's own good but the police then become not only the investigatory arm of the criminal-justice system, but also the judge and jury. On the other hand, not every criminal who claims he was the victim of a fit-up is telling the truth.)

Meanwhile, another unnamed underworld source told the *Daily Record*: 'The dogs on the street are shouting war. It's going to happen soon and people are going to get hurt . . . really hurt.'

Less than two days after speaking to the Scottish *Sun*, Bobby Glover was dead, his murder raising some uncomfortable questions for Glasgow Police. If he and Joseph Hanlon were 'target' criminals under suspicion for the Arthur Thompson murder – and apparently they were – then it is also almost certain that they would be under police observation. If that was the case, it would seem that the killer – or killers – had conveniently managed to spot a window in that observation to carry out their execution.

Some time after the double murders, the police admitted to the press that round-the-clock surveillance had been ordered on the two men – but that they had no idea of their movements on the night they died. They had somehow managed to evade their police shadows during the course of the evening. How they did so and where they went are just two of the unanswered questions still lingering over the case. It did emerge that Glover had arranged to meet someone at nine o'clock on the night he died. His friend, Joseph Hanlon, agreed to give him a lift to the rendezvous point because his own car was still in police hands. The man he was supposedly to meet was an old friend who was at that time on the run from prison.

Detectives travelled to London to investigate reports that a £50,000 contract had been put out on the two men, both of whom had been on the hit list young Arthur had been waving like a flag hours before he died. The usual unnamed underworld sources informed their favourite reporters that two London hit men had accepted the contract – and promised more killings. Meanwhile, another story was circulating that the hit man was of Asian origin with only one – white – accomplice. They had linked up with a Glasgow criminal, said to be the convict on the run, who arranged the meeting with Bobby Glover. This man, eventually named as William Lobban, denied any involvement in the murders. He had even been helped in his flight by Glover, he said. Lobban, jailed in 1988 for an armed robbery, had absconded from Dungavel prison near Strathaven in Lanarkshire in March 1991 while on special leave to visit a Glasgow clinic to have a tattoo removed. At one stage during his flight, he was said to be disguised as a woman, complete with make-up and a blonde wig, promptly being dubbed 'Tootsie' by press and criminals alike. Lobban was eventually recaptured during a joint operation by Strathclyde Police and officers of the Metropolitan Police. He has never been charged with any offences connected to the murders but in September 1993 was sentenced to six years for an armed robbery in a Glasgow pub, committed while he was on the run. Giving evidence against him was Eileen Glover, Robert's widow, who had tipped off the police in an act of revenge against the man she firmly believed was involved in her husband's death. During her testimony, Lobban said sadly: 'Eileen, Eileen. It wasn't me.'

There was another possibility mooted and circulated in the East End regarding the double killing: that the two had been silenced by their own side to prevent them from spilling their guts about the Thompson murder. A third theory buzzing around the city's criminals – who as always were showing a fine sense of rumour – was that they had actually been killed by a rogue police squad.

While all this was going on, the other men on young Arthur's legendary hit list were said to be living in terror of being the next to go. One of the men supposed to be on the list was at that time in the segregation unit of Barlinnie prison, where he was on remand for the Gillen shooting. The word was that he had been put there to protect him from Big Arthur's people but he himself insisted he was there because the authorities thought he was an escape risk. Then events took an unexpected but dramatic twist.

They hit Provanmill Road like the SAS, armed to the teeth and protected by body armour. A helicopter buzzed the air in the early morning September sunshine as powerful dogs tugged on leashes or sat, waiting patiently for their masters to give them the order to move. It was eight a.m. on Friday, 20 September 1991 and the police had decided it was time for a show of force, time to show the gangsters, hard men and drug dealers that they were still in charge of the city streets. And they had decided to do this by raiding the home of Big Arthur, the untouchable.

It was said later that the entire operation was a massive public-relations exercise, an attempt to reassure the ordinary citizens that the police were effective and offered no grace or favour to anyone, let alone the man they called the Godfather of Glasgow. The fact that they found nothing of any great evidential value in the expensive but well-publicised raid was neither here nor there. Strathclyde's finest had flexed their muscle.

The street was sealed off for nearly three hours, causing traffic chaos. Pedestrians were not allowed access from either end. Even home helps on their way to care for elderly charges were barred from going past. Journalists and photographers, who seemed to know about the raid in advance, were moved 200 yards away from the cordon, allegedly for their own safety. But if the police were fearful – or perhaps hoping – that the Thompson clan would shout something like 'Come and get us, you dirty coppers' à la James Cagney they were in for a disappointment.

The armed officers, some from the force's special armed-response unit, resplendent in their military-style jump-suits and snappy blue berets, hit the two Thompson houses from both sides. At the rear they picked their way through the gravestones of Riddrie cemetery, where young Arthur was buried, while at the front they stormed up in their vans, taking cover behind the low wall beside the pavement. Then the officers bearing search warrants moved to the front doors, one shouting to the late Arthur's brother: 'Put your hands above your head, Billy. We're coming towards the door.' Then they went in. Into both houses, later re-emerging with a hand-cuffed Billy Thompson, his father, mother and sister. They were placed in the backs of police vans while officers searched the houses and gardens. After that they turned their collective attention to the Thompson family cars and garages, impounding a white Vauxhall Astra. And then they left, later admitting that nothing of any significance had been found – although it would emerge in court that they had found a bullet-proof vest on the porch of one of the houses.

Soon after, Arthur Thompson's solicitor, Joseph Beltrami, announced that he had been instructed by his client to make a formal complaint to the chief constable regarding 'certain aspects of the police operation today'. Later that day, the police themselves held an unprecedented news conference, the aim of which was to let the drug barons know that while they were warring on each other, the police would also be warring on them.

Detective Chief Superintendent John Fleming, the man responsible for CID specialist services including criminal intel-ligence, told the reporters: 'The drugs trade in Glasgow is con-trolled by major toughened criminals. Very often they resort to acts of extreme violence to protect what they consider to be their jurisdiction and they strongly resent anyone trying to muscle in on their scene.' In speaking of the present violence he warned that there could be further deaths but assured the public that they were 99 per cent safe as long as the gangsters kept to their 'present methods'. It is known that criminal fig-ures do not like 'civilians' – ordinary citizens – becoming mixed up in their violent activities. If innocent bystanders are hurt, it generally brings down more heat than they can stand. As the American gangster Bugsy Segal once said about himself and his counterparts: 'We only kill each other.'

The top police officer said the targets knew they were in danger and that they had been warned in no uncertain terms of the risks they were taking. The detective even revealed he had personally warned both Hanlon and Glover the year before: 'Unless you get out of this scene then the next time I see you will be in the mortuary.' They ignored his warning, telling him to 'get on his bike'.

The police, DCS Fleming said, had been continually thwarted in their attempts to find the killers, often by members of the victims' own families. The word had gone out, it seems, that there was to be no co-operation with the police, that the matter would be dealt with by the dead men's associates. Meanwhile, other people had been assaulted but the victims, alive only through the skill of medical teams, refused to co-operate.

Police officers were seizing an increasing number of firearms from the city streets – 35 since January 1991. But as soon as they took one weapon out of circulation, another one took its place. Rival hoodlums were 'tooling up' for a blood-bath and as one ex-criminal said: 'There are guys getting guns out there that shouldn't be getting them. It used to be that guns were rare in Glasgow and you were careful who got them. But now they're frightened and they're giving them to anyone – including the psychos. And that's bloody dangerous.'

Jimmy Wray, MP for the Provan constituency which covered Arthur Thompson's street, threw in his comments, supporting the police efforts by calling for the public to help wherever they could. 'Mothers and fathers and brothers and sisters have to come forward and talk if we are to save lives from being lost – and I don't just mean from these shootings. Drug dealing causes so much misery. People in Glasgow don't traditionally "grass", but it is time they crossed that thin dividing line between right and wrong and came forward with evidence. Every single drug-related death should be plastered up in a big way so that people can see the scale of the problem we are dealing with.'

But at the same time, the MP asked the Secretary of State for Scotland to examine the actions of police officers during the raid on Arthur Thompson's home. He wanted to know why Mrs Rita Thompson had a gun held four inches from her head by a police officer; why Billy Thompson was taken away in handcuffs despite being termed merely as a witness; and why this supposedly secret police operation was known to an army of pressmen and photographers who were able to watch the proceedings and indeed report on them in full.

Arthur Thompson himself also broke his silence to the hated media, speaking to the *Daily Record* about the raid and lashing out angrily at the police officers who he said went over the top during the raid. 'They wanted me to come out with my hands over my head like something out of *Starsky and Hutch*,' he said, 'but there was no way because I saw the photographer waiting on the other side of the street. Then they wanted to handcuff me but I refused.' He continued: 'I want to make it clear that the CID behaved in a proper manner and I have no complaints about them. It is the gun-toting policemen I am unhappy about.'

The police announced that they would conduct an internal inquiry into the affair. Later the investigation would be taken over by the procurator fiscal's office and a report referred to the Crown Office who in June 1992 – after the murder trial – announced there would be no criminal proceedings against the officers involved. The news came as no surprise to anyone but, as Joseph Beltrami said: 'Mr Thompson did not ask that officers should be charged with any criminal offence. What he did ask for was an apology.'

In his interview with the *Daily Record*, Big Arthur also told those who made allegations that his dead son was a 'grass' to either put up or shut up. It was perhaps fitting that he laid this challenge down through the pages of the *Record* as it was their reporters who first made this tasty titbit public. 'Someone should say when he did it and give details of what he is supposed to have done,' the man said. 'It is easy to slander a dead person. This family is too strong to inform on anyone. I don't think there is any substance to the allegation that he was killed because he "grassed" on anyone because I know he didn't. But I don't know why he was killed.' Perhaps the old gangster was right. Perhaps his son did not inform on anyone. But no one believed that big Arthur did not know why his son was killed.

Thompson also spoke on television to BBC Scotland's Jackie Bird, calling her at intervals 'pet'. During the telephone interview he admitted publicly to being shot five years before and the fact that someone had tried to run him down. This was the first time he admitted being shot – he had always adhered to the flying drill-bit scenario. 'Now the police tell me my life is in danger – I think that's obvious,' he commented drily. He denied that he had refused to co-operate with the police in their investigations, saying he had no idea who shot his son and that there was no vendetta against the killers, calling for an end to the violence 'I've known the Hanlon family all their lives,' he said. 'The wee boy called "Bananas" I've known since he was three years old. I'm very sorry for their families.'

Meanwhile, according to the police, the wall of silence – what the Italians call *omerta* – surrounding the murders was crumbling. Also, the post-mortem had revealed that Hanlon and Glover had eaten Indian food on the night they were killed, so they surmised that they had visited an Indian restaurant, possibly for a carry-out. They searched an area around Hogganfield Loch, less than a mile away from Provanmill on the Cumbernauld Road northwards, where there was an Indian restaurant nearby and where one informant had told the police Hanlon had once stashed a shotgun. It later turned out that Glover's wife had cooked the curry for them.

In the meantime an anonymous caller had told the police that he had seen a man running from the rear of the Cottage bar at about seven on the night of the murder, then jump into the passenger side of a blue Ford Escort van which sped off in the direction of the city centre. Detectives were also still looking for a door handle from the blue Orion which they believe had been blown off by a bullet which hit the inside of the door. But they still did not know exactly where the men had been killed or how many killers were involved. The police also drove a blue Orion, similar to Hanlon's, into Darlieth Street in an attempt to jog the memories of any passers-by who had not yet contacted them. They claimed that 'a number of useful pieces of information were provided' as a result of the exercise. But obviously not enough.

Then came the dramatic revelation that Joseph Hanlon may well have tape recorded his murder. Although police would neither confirm nor deny its existence, it was believed that the man often carried a miniature tape recorder around with him. Like many other criminals, Hanlon lived in fear, whether real or imagined, of becoming the victim of a police 'fit-up' and so used this tiny device to secretly record conversations with police officers – or anyone else for that matter.

Hanlon's wife Sharon brought the existence of the recorder to the press's notice. 'I don't know that there is anything on it,' she told the *Herald*. 'I want to see justice done here. If there is anything on it that could bring these people – if you can call them that – to justice, that's what I want to see done.' She said she did not understand why the police were not making the tape public. 'I don't know why they don't say they've got it instead of printing things about drugs.' She and Hanlon's mother had already denied that the dead man had been involved in the drugs trade. 'He has never, ever been involved. I don't know where they got that from. He has never, ever been involved,' she emphasised. 'I can't bury my man,' she continued. 'I want to put him to rest now. As if I'm not going through enough. Why not now let me put him to rest?'

One man's name surfaced time and time again throughout these blood-soaked days. Paul Ferris, a one-time friend of young Arthur who had apparently been treated like a member of the family by Big Arthur, was the man being held in Barlinnie prison's segregation unit awaiting trial on the Gillen shooting charge. Naturally, word reached him that he was suspected of gunning down his one-time pal, prompting him to have his solicitor contact the *Daily Record* to strongly deny any involvement and also to debunk suggestions that he was being held in solitary because he was under threat from a gangland murder squad. In a fax to the newspaper, the lawyer stated his client was in segregation because he was regarded as a potential escapee by the authorities.

This was the second time Paul Ferris had been forced to publicly proclaim his innocence of Arthur Thompson's murder. Shortly after the slaying he spoke to the Scottish *Sun*, saying that he had gone into hiding in London because certain people had him marked down as an underworld hitman. He had, he said, left Glasgow before Thompson was shot and had returned three days after. 'I had differences of opinion in the past with Arthur,' he admitted, 'but I have absolutely no motive for doing what happened to him.'

Paul Ferris was 28 years of age when he was implicated in the murder. He had been brought up in Blackhill, reputedly one of the toughest areas in Glasgow and which had also spawned Arthur Thompson Snr and other hard men. It was also only a few hundred yards away from Arthur Thompson's lavish home. At one time, Mr Ferris had worked in the old man's garage but now he made a living selling cars and occasionally double-glazing. He and young Arthur had been close friends. When the latter went down for his 11 years, Paul Ferris often visited him in prison, even acting as chauffeur to allow Catherine, young Arthur's common-law wife, to see him.

But then something happened. There was a falling-out and a wedge was driven between the two – hence the reason for Ferris being suspected of the murder. According to one report, the friendship became strained when Ferris began to associate with a man believed to have been involved in the alleged fit-up of young Arthur. Slowly, word circulated around the East End that young Arthur's erstwhile pal had turned killer. Thugs, incensed (or perhaps ordered to be) at the man's alleged actions, knew they could not get at Ferris in Barlinnie's segregation unit, known as the Wendy House, where inmates are kept in solitary for 23 hours of the day. So they did the next best thing – they went for his family.

The first sign of trouble for 64-year-old William Ferris, Paul Ferris's father, was when his car tyres were slashed and acid was poured over the paintwork. But then it took a decidedly nasty turn.

On Saturday, 5 October 1991, as the elderly man was

making his way home from the pub, he was attacked by a gang of men armed with hammers. They jumped him outside his Blackhill home, battering him from behind, splitting his skull, before smashing his hands as he lay senseless. Then he was left for dead. On the same night, someone smashed windows at Arthur Thompson's home in nearby Provanmill Road. The police put it down officially to an attempted housebreaking. But who would dare to try something like that?

The first attack on William Ferris prompted Paul Ferris's girlfriend, Anne-Marie McCafferty, to appeal to the thugs through the pages of the Scottish *Sun* not to go after her or their six-year-old son, Paul. 'I know some people want to get wee Paul's dad. But nobody can get near him – so hurting his son is the obvious way of hurting him,' she said. 'It's really terrifying not knowing what the next knock at the door will bring. I cannot let my son grow up in fear.'

But that was not the end of William Ferris's troubles. By the end of the year he would be attacked again, the men coming at him out of the darkness once more as he made his way home from the pub, again hitting him from behind with a club and then falling on him, hacking and slashing at his face and head with a carpet knife. Later, doctors would put 46 stitches into his wounds.

The bodies of Bobby Glover and Joe Hanlon were finally released for burial. Glover's funeral, in Old Monkland cemetery in Coatbridge, was marred by an unpleasant incident involving a TV cameraman who was attacked by some of the mourners as he tried to film the proceedings. One mourner had earlier driven his car at a group of photographers gathering outside the cemetery. About 300 mourners followed the procession to the graveyard, where his wife, Eileen, left a wreath saying: 'I love you, Bobby. Goodnight darling. I'll never stop loving you.'

Hanlon's funeral took place in St Mungo's RC church in Townhead, Glasgow. Mourners travelled in over 50 cars and two buses. His brother, Paul, supported the widow, Sharon, as she wept uncontrollably throughout the 15-minute service.

At the graveside, they each threw a single red rose on to the coffin as it was lowered into the ground. Detectives were among the hundreds of mourners at both services, as is the custom in a murder inquiry.

Throughout the investigation, the tabloids continued to outdo each other with exclusives, often giving the impression that their reporters were conducting deeper inquiries than the police. On Friday 1 November the Scottish *Sun* told of the ordeal of one-time bank robber John Masterson who was allegedly kidnapped by two men at gunpoint in London and brought back to Scotland where the men questioned him about the deaths of Hanlon and Glover. Masterson was a friend of the Kray twins and had in fact campaigned for their release. The Krays, as has already been noted, were friendly with Arthur Thompson Snr. Masterson was grabbed off the street, a friend who was with him blinded by ammonia, and thrown into the back of a van. He later claimed he was held out of the van as it sped along the motorway and then had a gun barrel placed in his mouth and the trigger pulled. The gun was empty. Once back in Glasgow it seems the kidnappers took him blindfolded to a block of multi-storey flats and hung him bodily out of a window. Later, they drenched him in petrol and threatened to put a match to him. But they let him go. He staggered into the casualty unit of the Royal Infirmary, reeking of petrol and very badly shaken. After that, he refused to talk to detectives in Glasgow or London and the inquiries into his story ceased.

The same newspaper boasted yet another exclusive on 5 November, announcing that murder-squad detectives had found the getaway car used by young Arthur's killers. The stolen Nissan Bluebird had gone missing from the carpark of Hairmyres railway station in East Kilbride a few days prior to the murder. It was discovered again at Gartloch hospital near Easterhouse where it was on fire. An anonymous female caller reported the blaze to the police. But the story said that the police had refused to officially link the car with the murder.

And then on 6 November 1991, Paul Ferris was allowed

out on bail, telling reporters he was delighted to be out to spend Christmas with his son. The kneecapping charge still stood, however, and he still denied any involvement in either that incident or the Thompson murder. He would not be free for long.

Meanwhile, the police announced they were looking for three men – all on the run – in connection with the deaths of Hanlon and Glover. They did not say exactly what that connection was, merely that escaped prisoners William Lobban, Michael Healy and John Daly were dangerous and should not be approached by the public. All three denied they had anything to do with the killings. Bank robber Michael Healy, an ex-French Foreign legionnaire, even said from a hideaway that 'you couldn't pay me in gold to shoot any man in the back'. He also scotched any rumours that he had in fact murdered William Lobban to keep him quiet. Lobban himself turned up alive and well when he was recaptured in London during January 1992. He had been on the run for an amazing ten months. And although he and the other two men were later named in a special defence of incrimination by Paul Ferris, they have never been charged by the police in connection with any of the events detailed here.

Paul Ferris's taste of freedom was short-lived. He was picked up again by police and appeared in Glasgow sheriff court on 25 November to be charged with the murder of Arthur Thompson Jnr. Hanlon and Glover were also named on the charge. The accused man made no plea and was remanded in custody for further inquiries. He would not be spending Christmas with his son after all.

What was to become Scotland's longest-running murder trial began on Monday, 23 March 1992 in the High Court of Glasgow. It would last a total of 54 days and the jury in the famous North Court, which has heard many a complex tale, were regaled with a succession of witnesses who brought into public scrutiny the methods and dirty dealings of the city's underworld – an organised criminal society which many citizens would rather believe does not exist.

The trial, before Lord McCluskey, would prove controversial and dramatic. Extra security measures were introduced. Spectators heading for the public gallery were met at the top of the stairs by uniformed police officers and searched with the aid of metal detectors. As an added precaution, the first two rows of benches in the public gallery were roped off, blocking a clear view of the court so that all that spectators could see were the witness box, the judge and the jury of eight women and seven men (although one of the female jurors had to be excused midway through the proceedings because of illness).

Paul Ferris was represented by Donald Findlay QC, a modern legend in Scottish courts. Ironically, he had defended Arthur Thompson Jnr during his drugs trial – and would later defend William Lobban on his armed-robbery charge. Prosecuting in the Ferris trial was Advocate-depute Roderick MacDonald QC.

The accused faced ten charges in total including, of course, the murder of Arthur Thompson Jnr. The charge alleged that he had acted in this along with Robert Glover and Joseph Hanlon. He was also accused of attempting to murder William Gillen, along with Robert Glover, as well as attempting to murder another man who was shot in the neck in Rutherglen. There were other charges of attempting to pervert the course of justice, conspiring to assault another man and possession of controlled drugs and guns. The accused man denied all the charges, lodging special defences of alibi and incrimination.

In the early weeks, the public gallery was packed. There was a preponderance of hard-faced men, chib marks to the fore and more tattoos than Edinburgh in August. They sat forward in the benches, faces set in hard lines as they listened intently to the testimony of the succession of witnesses standing in the box below. And so the drama began.

The trial was halted almost as soon as it started. It was on the second day, while the court was hearing evidence from witnesses regarding the attempted murder of Arthur Thompson

Snr, that Donald Findlay drew the judge's attention to what he believed was a potentially very serious situation for his client, Paul Ferris. In a news bulletin on BBC2 in Scotland at 3.55 p.m. on Monday – the first day of the trial – viewers were shown a three-second-long piece of film of the accused being led into court in which the man's face could be clearly seen. As the question of identification could be critical during evidence, that short piece of film was, in the QC's opinion, one of the most 'serious *prima facie* contempts of court' he had ever seen. 'It shows not only what effectively amounts to a series of photographs of the accused,' he said, 'it shows him being brought out of a police van in handcuffs. He could not be more clearly identified in any way.'

The following day, Lord McCluskey found the BBC in contempt of court, saying: 'It is clearly essential that witnesses are not materially influenced in any way. It follows that, in any case where the question of identification may arise, it is clear that the publication in the press or television of any film, photograph or even an artist's likeness during a trial or after a warrant has been issued causes a potential risk to the administration of justice.' It was the first time the BBC had been accused of contempt of court since it began broadcasting in Scotland in 1927. Lord McCluskey took this impeccable record into account when he gave his judgment on the contempt at the end of the trial and admonished the Corporation. He would not be so lenient with a newspaper also found in contempt over an article which followed Arthur Thompson's testimony.

From all accounts, the testimony of the so-called Godfather of Glasgow was a tour-de-force. He bandied words with Donald Findlay, peppering his evidence with his customary one-liners. Even the judge smiled occasionally.

Advocate-depute Roderick MacDonald asked Thompson how he was sometimes described in the press. 'Bank robber, hooligan, various other things,' he replied.

'Have you sometimes been referred to as the Godfather?'

'I'll tell you what happened,' Thompson began to explain, 'Mr Beltrami, the lawyer, wrote a book which was serialised in the *Evening Times*. It referred to Patrick Meehan who was sentenced to life imprisonment after the police framed him for something he did not do. Mr Beltrami kept saying to people whether Meehan was guilty or innocent and at the end of the day Mr Beltrami got in touch with me. He said to me: "Arthur, what is the score? Was Meehan involved?" I said to him: "The dogs in the street know who done it. Meehan did not do it."' In his book, the lawyer was going to refer to Thompson as the Godfather. Arthur Thompson asked him not to. He claimed there was no truth in the rumour that he was some sort of Godfather.

'You are sometimes described as a gang leader?' asked the advocate-depute.

'Sir, I am 61 years of age, not 21 years of age!' He did admit, though, to a number of convictions, including assault and robbery, safeblowing and extortion. Later he admitted being well known throughout Glasgow pointing out that he had 'more cousins than Hitler had an army – everyone claims to know me'. He described the hit-and-run attempt on his life, denying he had fired a gun at the car when he saw the vehicle careering towards him – and explaining why he did not inform the police of the incident. 'I have lost faith in the police,' he said. 'I do not believe in them one bit.'

He claimed his son had been framed by the police on the drugs charges ('The police planted evidence and fitted him up. The police are responsible for where he is today'). The police, he said, were 'bent' and some witnesses 'slags' ('If you were a dog born with AIDS you would not want to know him,' he said of one), and described the events of the night young Arthur was murdered ('Some cowardly bastard shot him in the back before he could get to the house'). Of the accused, Paul Ferris, he said: 'I did not have much to do with him. He was an associate of my son, Arthur. He was a pal of my son.'

He also spoke of the raid on his home two days after his son's funeral. At about seven in the morning he heard a commotion outside his house and heard a voice shouting: 'Arthur, Arthur, open up.' He pulled open his curtain and looked out and saw a helicopter outside and policemen in the street shouting: 'Come out, come out.'

'I went down to the front door with a pullover and shirt over my arm. Armed police said "don't move". I asked if I could put my shirt on and one said yes but another said "put your hands in the air". I said they should get their act together.' There were armed police on either side of him and he asked why they were holding him and they said in case he ran away. 'I said there are 70 armed policemen with rifles and handguns pointing at me so I wasn't likely to run.'

Although he was currently claiming sickness benefit he insisted his business interests included a car showroom in Maryhill and renovation companies in the Gorbals and Shettleston. He denied ever owning pubs or clubs. When talking about allegations that he earned £100,000 a week from loan-sharking operations, he scoffed: 'This is a joke. It also says a man was nailed to the door of a garage by a crucifix. There is no foundation to this.

'It is just the press,' he said, 'it is pure lies.'

Donald Findlay asked: 'Do you dispute the allegation that you are a criminal overlord in Glasgow?'

'Of course I dispute it. It is a lot of nonsense.'

Naturally, he rejected any suggestion that his son was involved in the drugs trade, either in or out of prison. He also denied reports that young Arthur had been seen with guns and ammunition just prior to his death. He also said he did not know what a bullet-proof vest was, even when shown the one found on the porch of his son's home during the police raid. 'I have never seen one before,' he said. 'It looks like a vest the police wore when they come to my door. But it doesn't say police on it.' He then claimed he could not think of any reason why his family would have a bullet-proof vest. He did not know why his son had adverts for handguns and body armour pasted into an album which also contained pictures of the Thompson family with Paul Ferris. For a living legend, Big Arthur really did not know very much. 'I don't know of any reason why my son should be interested in purchasing a gun or body armour,' he insisted. 'His only interest in armoury was guns from battleships like the *Hood* and the *Bismark*.'

Then he was questioned regarding his alleged involvement in the deaths of Hanlon and Glover. 'If I suggest you orchestrated or arranged the shooting of Glover and Hanlon in revenge for the death of your son, what do you say to that?' Mr Findlay asked.

'I would say that I think I'm on trial here, the way you are going on. That is the dock,' Arthur Thompson replied, pointing to where Paul Ferris sat. 'This is the witness box.' He said he bore the men no malice and did not think they were responsible for his son's death. Later, he said: 'We all know who shot him. We think so.' This last statement was made when Donald Findlay was exploring the suggestion that the man behind the murder of Thompson Jnr was not Ferris but another of the dead man's former associates who allegedly had his own plans for taking over the city's drugs trade. This man had been accused with Thompson Jnr on the drugs charges but had received only six years.

Arthur Thompson left the witness box with his reputation intact. Despite being a witness for the prosecution, he had managed to avoid implicating anyone directly yet still making it clear who he held responsible. He may not have been the prosecution's star witness – he would come later – but he was undoubtedly a star.

It was this interest in the man which landed *Scotland on Sunday* in trouble with Lord McCluskey. On 29 March they published a highly readable and hugely entertaining article detailing some of the background of the case as it referred to Thompon's testimony. Again, it was the ever-vigilant Donald Findlay – stalwartly protecting his client's interests – who drew it to the judge's attention on 1 April claiming the story contained a number of assertions about matters of fact which appeared not to be matters of fact at all. In their contempt hearing, again at the end of the trial, Lord McCluskey fined the newspaper, reporter and editor a total of £3,500.

After Arthur Thompson left the stand, the jury was treated to a parade of witnesses who were doing their best to implicate Paul Ferris in the crimes – and rebuttal witnesses who painted a different picture of much of their testimony. As Lord McCluskey commented to the jury at the end of the mammoth affair: 'In this long trial you have listened to an extraordinary catalogue of lies and deceit, cruelty and death.'

Hanging over it all was the spectre of the drugs trade. Yet the majority of the witnesses claimed to despise the business. It was dirty, they would say, and we have nothing whatsoever to do with it. A number of them admitted to having horrendous records. One or two, if they were to be believed, were so virtuous they made Mother Theresa look like a Mafia capo.

A self-confessed drug user, liar and perjurer claimed that Paul Ferris offered him money to kill Arthur Thompson Jnr. Another witness said he had been shot in the neck through the window of his flat. The court heard of Joseph Hanlon's ice-cream van being petrol bombed and how the man himself was shot in the penis during the attack. His car was also petrol bombed. William Gillen gave a horrific account of his kneecapping, claiming that Paul Ferris and others had accused him of 'messing them around' over certain information. The shooting was meant as a 'message'.

A female witness harked back to the notorious 1984 ice-cream war trial when she claimed she had been pressurised by the police into making false statements. She said a police officer had frightened her into incriminating Ferris by reminding her about that earlier trial, which dealt with the murder of six people in their home during a fire attack, saying that 'her weans will fry' if she did not speak up. In court, she refused to stand by her statement. Her common-law husband also spoke of veiled threats if he did not speak against the accused. Another witness said he had been forced to make a statement by a relative who said he would be slashed if he did not.

A letter addressed to Paul Ferris purporting to be from the Crown Office also contributed to yet another bizarre line of inquiry. Copies of the letter, on what looked like official headed notepaper, had been circulating around Glasgow pubs and even pushed through letterboxes. One witness, who could corroborate Paul Ferris's whereabouts on the night

William Gillen was shot, said he had found the letter through his door one day. The poorly written and greatly misspelt letter, dated 12 February 1992, was addressed to Mr Paul Ferris, Reg. No 7684/91, HM Prison, Barlinnie, Glasgow and read as follows:

Dear Sir,
I refer to the letter of 12 January 1992 (sent on your behalf) which was passed to the Lord Advocate who ackowledge's (*sic*) the assistance given by you to the Stathclyde (*sic*) Serious Crime Squad over several years.

However, inquires (*sic*) have shown that your prior assistance was for 'Monetary Consideration' and not 'Public Spirited'. Accordingly the Lord Advocate feels unable to intervene in the matters outstanding against you.
Yours faithfully,
Mr A. Vannet, Deputy Crown Agent.

The intention was clear: the letter implied that Paul Ferris was a 'grass' for the serious crime squad and had been, for some time, receiving payments for informing on others. Information like this, if believed, would go very badly for a man, especially in prison where grasses are not the most popular of people. The letter however, was an obvious forgery. The spelling was the first and most noticeable problem. Also, as the court heard, Crown Office paper of that size is light blue and not white, while Mr Alfred Vannet, the supposed writer of the letter, testified that the signature was not his (he signed letters A.D. Vannet) and in his opinion someone had taken the official letterhead and photocopied it on top of the forged letter.

Another item of correspondence, this time a postcard, was also shown in court. This was addressed to Arfur Thomsin, c/o The Guv, HMP Noranside, Scotland, and dated 22 July 1991. It read:

Hi Arf,
Did you hear Ron's getting a house in Scotland? Yea, Aberdeen. So you will be all right on the out. But keep it to

yourself. Be lucky. You'l (*sic*) need it.
Reg and Ron.

The card was postmarked London N1 6.15 p.m. and was deemed to be from the Kray brothers. A police handwriting expert would testify that in his opinion that card was written by Paul Ferris. Why is not clear.

Yet another letter had already been read out, this time from a prisoner in Barlinnie to his girlfriend regarding his proposed involvement in the trial. The prisoner was known in Scotland as Denis Woodman, but was known in parts of England under other names. The letter was written to his wife, Fiona, and talked about Arthur Thompson Snr.

In it he said: 'Do you know who Arthur Thompson is? He's the fucking godfather of Glasgow . . . he's a fucking gangster. The top one in Glasgow . . .' While the letter was being read out in court during Arthur Thompson's testimony, the witness interrupted at this point saying: 'The man is a fucking looney.' The letter continued: 'Did Ferris's pals tell you that Thompson is on our fucking side, Fiona? You'll want for nothing. I did it for you, you stupid fool. You give me an answer. If you don't want me to give evidence, I won't. But fucking tell me now before the trial starts. Yes, I never did grass your dad, so pack that in, right? To hell with the fucking trial. Ferris can wait and give the money to whoever you want. To fuck with Ferris and the trial. I am no longer a Crown witness. You'll have the money before Thursday. Ferris can go to fuck . . .'

Arthur Thompson's view on the man was that he was 'a nut. He wanted this letter to come here as a production.' Donald Findlay suggested that the money referred to in the letter was for false evidence against Paul Ferris, to which Thompson replied: 'On my son's death, the man is a liar.' The subject of whether Woodman was lying or not would come up again when the man himself took the stand – and in doing so fatally damaged the Crown case against Paul Ferris. For it became increasingly obvious that the man was indeed a liar – and the suggestion was that he had been planted in prison beside Ferris to help manufacture evidence against him, although this was strongly denied by the authorities.

At around this time *Scotland on Sunday* found itself in more legal trouble but this time not with Lord McCluskey. Arthur Thompson announced his intention to sue the paper for defamation after publication of two articles which strongly suggested that he was a crime kingpin. At this time, practically everyone in Glasgow and even beyond knew that Big Arthur was one of the most powerful criminal overlords the city had ever seen – but heaven help anyone who said so in print. As it had never been proved in court, he was euphemistically described as a 'Glasgow businessman'.

In announcing his client's intention to sue, Thompson's solicitor said: 'My client has made it clear to the newspaper that he considers both articles to be grossly defamatory in that they suggested his involvement in crime and organised crime in particular. He is, of course, involved in neither.' The statement was met by snorts of derision in pubs throughout the East End – and not a few newsrooms. Later, Thompson accepted a four-figure sum in an out-of-court settlement, half of which was given to Radio Clyde's Cash for Kids appeal.

The financial problems of the late Joseph Hanlon were explored during the testimony of his common-law wife, Sharon. She told the court that he was a charge-hand at the Caravel public house in Barlanark, earning approximately £400 a month. He supplemented his income by running an ice-cream van purchased on a bank loan for £16,000. The run brought him in just enough to keep up the loan payments. Later, the Crown's star witness, the aforementioned Dennis Woodman, would state that Hanlon sold heroin from that ice-cream van. The van in question was firebombed in Ruchazie in 1991 and about four months later his car was blown up. In addition, Hanlon himself was shot in the penis and he lost his job. Life was far from being a bed of roses for Joseph Hanlon, it seems.

The witness told the court that on the night Arthur Thompson Jnr was killed she had met Hanlon coming up the stairs of their close at about 7.15 p.m.. He told her that he was going to have a bath and then go to work at the pub. When she arrived home at about 11.45 p.m., he was in the house. When she heard the following day from gossip in the shops that young Arthur had been killed, she returned home and asked Hanlon if he knew. He replied: 'How the fuck am I supposed to know?' She said that he did not seem to be too interested in the murder. On the night of his own death, Sharon Hanlon had seen him last at about 9.15 p.m. when he left the house. She believed he was going to meet Robert Glover, who had phoned earlier.

Robert Glover's wife, Eileen, testified that he had been with her at an engagement party between 11 p.m. and two a.m. on the night of the Thompson killing. She said she knew William Lobban and that he had stayed in their home for three months while on the run. When Lobban had fled to London, Glover had given him a couple of hundred pounds.

A convicted car thief took the stand to tell the court that he had been offered 'a monkey' – £500 – to burn the car that had been allegedly used in the murder. He said he had been offered the cash by Robert Glover, who ultimately only paid him £100 of the sum agreed. He said he had earlier stolen the car from the station carpark at East Kilbride for William Lobban. After he had set the car on fire in the grounds of Gartloch hospital, he was picked up by Robert Glover who dismissed his reports of the car not going very well with: 'That was that fucking Joe's driving.' The inference was that Joseph Hanlon had driven the car on the night of the murder. In October 1991, the witness heard that police were looking for him in connection with the murder and he went to London Road police office with his solicitor to answer their questions. He said they told him that he might be the next one to be shot and he told them what he knew. At the time of the trial he was under police protection. At the time he gave his statement to the police, he was also wanted in connection with a bank robbery. He was charged with this, remanded in custody for three weeks and then released. He had been told there would be 'no further proceedings'.

Then came the evidence of Dennis Woodman. The Englishman had been in Dumfries Prison on remand for charges of kidnapping and extortion. The authorities had apparently received information that he was likely to try and escape and when his cell was searched they found a small quantity of drugs, a pistol made out of cardboard and a small saw blade. They decided to move the man to Barlinnie for security reasons.

The authorities should have known that while in England he had given evidence as a 'grass'. Woodman, better known as Wilkinson, was in fact a supergrass and had helped the police put away a number of people, on occasion by claiming that he had been told things by the various accused while in prison with them. Just as he was about to do with Paul Ferris.

While in the segregation unit at Barlinnie – the Wendy House – Woodman apparently played chess with Paul Ferris, who had been resident there from the beginning of September to mid-November. The game was played by prisoners shouting moves to each other from cell to cell. It was these games which would form the core of Woodman's testimony. But before he took the stand, a Barlinnie prison governor told the court that he had warned Woodman he was putting his life in danger by telling other prisoners he was going to testify against the accused. The governor said he had no knowledge of Woodman's previous exploits in England.

Then Woodman himself took the stand. The spotlight would be on him for five days. Five days of allegations, of shouted conversations in the segregation unit, of confessions, of bribes, of threats, of stories of drugs and death. Very little of it rings true.

Woodman, his demeanour arrogant, his evidence not just unbelievable but occasionally downright ludicrous, was seen to smile broadly at Paul Ferris and point his finger at him, giving a lie to the fears he had expressed to the judge, Lord McCluskey. 'My Lord,' he began soon after climbing into the witness box, 'I am in a strange position here. I am in prison and at the moment I fear for my life because of Mr Ferris. I am just at the moment too frightened to say much because of what might happen to me. The Crown have to ensure the protection I need.' This was rich, considering he had been telling prisoners what he planned to do. And from all reports, he did not appear in court to be a man who was in fear of his life. Unless, of course, he possessed supreme self-control and was able to hide his fear from the public. The judge told him he must answer the questions and that he could not deal with the matter.

During his testimony, he explained that his real name was Wilkinson but it was changed in 1986 to Jones after he gave evidence for the police in an English case. It was changed again, with stunning originality, to Smith after someone tried to shoot him in a carpark. In 1988 it was changed finally to Woodman. He was asked if this was because there was a contract out on him and he replied: 'There are a lot of contracts out on me.'

He would admit he had made a statement ten years before claiming that he had been blackmailed by police and pressurised into giving evidence at five big English trials. However, he had made that statement, he claimed, because associates of one of the men against whom he had testified had kidnapped his wife and mother and was holding them captive in a London hotel. He had given evidence at six English trials. It would have been more but he had been working undercover for the police in other cases, he said. He finally admitted that he had been paid 'a few grand' for his work.

At one of the English trials, the court heard from a police witness, Woodman had given evidence against a man accused of various armed robberies. His testimony dealt with various conversations Woodman/Wilkinson had with the accused man while they were both on remand. His testimony in the Glasgow case would also deal with conversations conducted while in prison. Woodman, at the time serving eight years for conspiracy to rob and other charges, also claimed that a deal had been struck with the procurator fiscal in Glasgow to get him into a lower-category prison in return for his testimony. The advocate-depute would take that up with him, saying that only his safety had been guaranteed as far as possible. 'I came to court to tell the truth,' said Woodman. 'I am telling you that a bargain was struck – it is not an inducement, it is common sense.'

Occasionally the exchanges, particularly between Woodman and Donald Findlay, became quite heated. After one angry reply, in which Woodman used the word 'bloody', he was told by the judge: 'In order to allow the jury to assess what kind of person you are I have allowed you to shout and swear in the witness box but this is the last time I will issue you with a simple warning. Any more of your foul mouth, shouting hooliganism and I will find you guilty on the spot of contempt of court and punish you.'

During his period in the segregation unit, Woodman said that Paul Ferris told him – a complete stranger – just about everything the police would want to know. He said Ferris had told him that Arthur Thompson Snr was the Godfather of Glasgow and that young Arthur had taken over the drugs business in Glasgow. 'He told me he had decided to kill the son, Arthur Thompson Jnr,' said Woodman. 'On the night there went with him Joe Hanlon and Bobby Glover who were his trusted mates, and they waited for him coming into the street and they shot him in the back. This happened in Provanmill Road.' It was Paul Ferris who pulled the trigger, said the witness. Later, he said Ferris hated the Thompsons. 'He said he would kill Arthur Thompson Snr if he got the chance. He was going to blow his house up.'

Mr Ferris had also confessed, it seemed, to dealing in heroin and cocaine and could set Woodman up in the drugs business if he pleaded not guilty and got off. Remember, this was a complete stranger whom Paul Ferris could not even see: this information was being shouted from one cell to another. Woodman said that Mr Ferris had told him that Hanlon and Glover had been killed on the orders of Arthur Thompson Snr. He had paid either the Triads (Chinese gangsters) or Lobban and Healy.

Obviously not content with telling this man about the murder, Paul Ferris also felt compelled to confess his involvement in the shooting of William Gillen. 'He told me that he

181

and a couple of his mates had driven Gillie to Loganwell because he had ripped them off on some drug money,' Woodman stated. He went on to say that Paul Ferris had originally intended to kill the man but had decided to just shoot him in the legs because he thought he heard a car coming. Surely though, if he heard a car, he would have abandoned the idea of firing the gun at all.

Woodman then accused Ferris of putting a £400,000 price tag on his head. 'The things he has done to try and stop me coming here you just would not believe,' he said. Ultimately, the jury did not believe much of what Woodman was saying anyway, so he might as well have told them. He also denied giving evidence in return for parole. 'I asked the police for nothing,' he claimed. 'I said just make sure I don't get thrown beside rapists and sex offenders.' He later said he was now in solitary confinement because he was giving evidence. 'I am here to tell the truth because I am finished with crime,' he said.

But Donald Findlay was unimpressed. Almost from the beginning of his cross-examination he went on the attack. The pair clashed frequently and insultingly, with Woodman calling the QC a fool and even a liar. At one point he even commented that he would love to get in a boxing ring with Mr Findlay. 'No doubt you would, Mr Woodman,' said Donald Findlay.

At another point in the trial, Woodman said he had once faced five QCs in an English case and they were a lot better than Mr Findlay. 'You may be the top dog in Scotland but not down south,' he accused.

'Don't flatter me, Mr Woodman,' replied the distinguished QC.

Not content with trying to implicate the accused in everything from the killing of Arthur Thompson Jnr to the kneecapping of William Gillen, Woodman also claimed that Paul Ferris's solicitor had offered him £60,000 and £20,000 a year for life if he would forget what he had heard in the segregation unit. 'I wanted no part of his drugs or murders. His mate had an ice-cream van pushing drugs to little children at street corners,' he alleged. This was a reference to Joseph

Hanlon and the common belief in Glasgow that gangsters run ice-cream vans in the city's schemes and sell drugs along with the ice-cream cones. (This belief, basically a myth, gained currency during the aforementioned ice-cream murders trial of 1984 – a trial which has many parallels with the Ferris case – and was promoted as fact by certain reporters. In the weeks following the deaths of Hanlon and Glover – before any arrests were made – at least one paper reprinted the allegations. There is little foundation to the rumours, although there have been isolated instances of traders dealing certain drugs from the back of ice-cream vans. However, it is not as widespread as these reporters would have their readers believe. As one former drug baron commented: 'Where the fuck would you stash the stuff on a van? And what would you do if the police gave you a pull and decided to turn you over [search the van]? You certainly couldn't make a high-speed getaway in one of they fucking things!')

Woodman claimed that for one meeting with this solicitor he was fitted with a concealed tape recorder to try and trap the man. But he said prison officers bungled the attempt and made it look too obvious so the alleged target, suspecting something, just stared at Woodman for a long period of time without saying anything in the slightest way incriminating. In the recording, played in court, nothing was said that sounded as if the solicitor was trying to trick Woodman. Neither did the man sound anxious or in any way concerned. 'I knew he had tippled what was going on,' said Woodman.

'To try to ruin a man's professional reputation is dishonest, damnable and downright evil,' thundered Mr Findlay.

'He was covering up his tracks,' Woodman insisted. In fact, the solicitor, who had an impeccable reputation, had gone to see Woodman to take a statement from him regarding his testimony in the trial. The statement, what is known as a precognition, had been refused on other occasions. It was not the first time that Woodman had made similar accusations against a solicitor. He had once claimed that an English lawyer offered him £10,000 to make false statements regarding his client, against whom Woodman was testifying.

Donald Findlay put it to Woodman that he had gleaned much of his information about the Thompson murder from newspaper reports of the murders. Woodman said he was in Dumfries prison at the time and had no interest in the story. He also claimed that his two children were dead, at one point swearing on their ashes he was telling the truth. But later in the trial his ex-wife gave evidence, telling the court his children were in fact alive and well. Eventually, the QC took off the gloves, which had been only lightly worn up until then, and went for the man verbally. 'You have been motivated by malice and self-interest in order to get something out of it for Number One, David Dennis Woodman. You are willing to blacken the name and character of anyone involved, the accused, lawyers, prison officers, who get in the way of your own selfish ends.' He continued: 'In the many, many years that this witness box and its predecessors have stood in this High Court of Justiciary in Glasgow, aren't you the biggest liar ever to disgrace its existence?'

'That's not true,' replied Woodman. In the end, though, the jury did not believe him.

Eventually, it was Paul Ferris's turn to take the stand in his own defence, his performance rivalling that of Arthur Thompson. When the advocate-depute described two of the witnesses against him as potential stooges, the accused added: 'And Woodman, then you would have three stooges.' One of the other witnesses, who claimed the accused had hired him to kill someone, was described as a 'deranged junkie'. He said the witness would be the last person anyone would ask to become a hit man. 'He is a heroin addict, and for him to be a hired gunman is sheer fantasy,' he said. Another witness, he said, had 'overdone his script a bit when he jerked his finger in my direction'.

The advocate-depute accused him of dealing in drugs. 'That is how you finance the lavish lifestyle you had last year and the year before,' he alleged. The accused insisted that he was a car dealer dealing in expensive vehicles, saying: 'You obviously have the same attitude as the police. The police accused me of being involved in drugs and fabricated charges against me.' That was why he fled to London, he said, to avoid the fit-up. But he did not have enough money to stay in London and had returned. He claimed William Gillen was only naming him to receive money from the Criminal Compensation Board.

Of Woodman he said: 'I wouldn't want to see any man in prison – except Woodman. It's a mental hospital he should be in anyway.' He said later in his testimony: 'I don't think there are enough words in the English vocabulary that could adequately describe someone as sick as that.' He had never spoken to Woodman, either in prison or out and his evidence was 'total fabrication'. He had never played chess with the man and in response to a question about a prison officer's testimony regarding overhearing the men shouting out moves he explained that Woodman had been playing another prisoner and Ferris had become involved in a dispute over the intricacies of castling.

Meanwhile, Arthur Thompson Jnr was dismissed in this way: 'If he had not lived in his father's reputation he would have been regarded as a stand-up comedian.' He told the court he had feared the police would kill him after the Thompson shooting. 'Police don't come to your door and say they want to speak to you,' he said. 'They kick open the door and, if you happen to go to the door with a TV remote control in your hand, someone might have an itchy finger and blow you away. Later their excuse would be that he appeared to have a firearm.' He claimed detectives had once arrived at his home with guns in their hands and that it was only due to his girlfriend's presence that 'something unfortunate didn't happen'. He said he had not killed Arthur Thompson Jnr – that he had been in the Caravel pub at the time – nor had he shot William Gillen or anyone else. Again he had alibis and also incriminated others. After five days on the stand he returned to the dock. There were a couple of other witnesses to be heard – one of whom placed himself in danger of contempt when he refused to name a heroin dealer in court – and then it was all over bar the shouting.

The shouting, figuratively speaking, would come from

the two opposing counsel in their closing arguments. The advocate-depute began his remarks by commenting on the sheer length of the trial.

'On Monday 23 March this year, when you were empanelled to serve on this jury, as winter was drawing to an end you each took an oath to well and truly try the accused and to give a true verdict according to that evidence. Since that time spring has come and summer has arrived [this was 8 June] and throughout the entire period since 23 March you have listened to a vast amount of evidence covering many matters and different incidents.' He went on to say that the question of whether some of the many witnesses had told the truth 'loomed very large'. In insisting that Paul Ferris was guilty of drug dealing, he pointed to the accused's lifestyle of travelling in aeroplanes and taxis and living in London hotels; a lifestyle that did not seem to have any visible means of support. The accused had claimed he was a car dealer but had not produced one person to whom he had sold a car. In 1991, he pointed out, he had only earned between three and four thousand pounds. Also in his testimony, Mr Ferris had described heroin as a scourge but the advocate-depute said that could be regarded not just as lies but as hypocrisy. As for the murder of Arthur Thompson Jnr, who was a convicted dealer, this could be seen as an attempt by Ferris to protect his interest. The lawyer said: 'It is a reasonable conclusion to come to, that if the accused was living from income obtained by the supplying of controlled drugs, that it is something he would seek to defend and he would not want any competition to destroy that.' The Crown case was, he conceded, circumstantial but when the pieces of evidence were taken together they formed a strand that should be sufficient for the jury to convict Paul Ferris for murder.

Paul Ferris's QC also commented on the extreme length of the trial, saying: 'The seasons have come and gone, a General Election has been won and lost, according to your point of view, and royal marriages have waxed and waned.' Donald Findlay's response to the question of his client's earnings the previous year was that he had been in jail for most of that time. The advocate-depute had referred to the lilies in the field when discussing Paul Ferris, saying that he 'neither toiled nor did he spin'. Mr Findlay asked: 'How was a man supposed to toil and spin if he was locked up in Barlinnie . . . ?' He disputed the evidence of Ferris's luxurious lifestyle, pointing out that when he returned to Glasgow from London he had to borrow the cash to buy a school uniform for his son. Woodman was an unreliable witness whose testimony should be ignored, he said, while one man who had been named in connection with the William Gillen shooting had not been called to give evidence, despite being on the Crown's witness list. 'If you leave a gap like that, it is too much to ask you to ignore it,' he said.

The judge said the jury were entitled to accept or reject parts of Woodman's evidence, saying 'even the worst of liars can tell the truth sometimes'. In the matter of witnesses who might have been called, he noted that their absence goes 'unexplained'. He said: 'You must decide if their absence is of such importance that you cannot come to a proper conclusion.' He said the accused had admitted to a variety of offences, including drug taking, being on the fringe of resetting and had been in prison. But these could not be held against him. This case, said Lord McCluskey, was about murder, appalling violence and serious drug dealing. He pointed out that Mr Ferris's evidence had been clear and articulate and that the charge of drug supplying was the common thread which held all the others together.

On the 53rd day of the murder trial – Lord McCluskey's 63rd birthday – the jury retired to consider their verdict. They took almost 24 hours to reach their decision, filing back into the North Court at 3.30 p.m. on Friday, 12 June 1992. Paul Ferris stood in the dock, smartly dressed, his fresh face marred only by the scar on his right cheek. He appeared calm, almost nonchalantly sucking a sweet, ready to heed his QC's advice to keep his dignity no matter what the verdict.

The clerk asked the spokesman for the jury if they had reached their verdicts and he said: 'Yes.' They had found Paul Ferris not guilty by a majority on the first four charges. As they said not guilty to the third charge the packed public gallery, unable to control their collective emotions, began to grow excited. They exploded with applause as the verdict to the fifth charge, the murder of Arthur Thompson Jnr, was delivered – not guilty by unanimous decision. Paul Ferris, relief clearly draining his strength, was also found not guilty of the remaining two charges. Donald Findlay turned and shook his erstwhile client's hand, telling him to take care of himself. The judge thanked the jury, saying 'it has been a privilege for me to see a case conducted with such fairness, thoroughness and skill.' He then went on to say that it was plain that they had 'wholly rejected the evidence of Woodman in relation to the murder charge'. Donald Findlay later said that the verdict was a clear vindication of the Scottish jury system. He commended the jurors for being able to understand the complexities of the case and for delivering verdicts based solely on the evidence they had heard in the courtroom.

Outside that courtroom, Paul Ferris basked in a hero's welcome. Over 300 supporters gathered in jail square, cheering and applauding as he stepped into the summer sunshine a free man. He called immediately for a public inquiry into the use of Woodman at his trial.

No such inquiry has ever taken place. The authorities in Scotland do not like to wash such dirty linen in public. It is doubtful if they have even been given a quick rinse in private. They would much rather that it is ignored and then perhaps it would go away. However, there was a strong feeling, expressed by lawyers and journalists, that the Crown had made a serious mistake in using a man who had apparently heard more confessions than a priest at Lent. That he is a proven liar there can be no doubt – but he was not the only one to take the stand during the 12 weeks. That the authorities knew he was a liar and used him anyway is a matter for conjecture. If they knew about his past then they committed a grave error of judgment in allowing him to take the stand. If they did not, then they allowed him to speak without checking his background. Either way, questions should not only have been asked but also answered. And we're still waiting.

The way the case was handled evokes strong memories of an earlier Glasgow murder trial, already mentioned in connection with this case – the ice-cream wars trial. In 1984, two men, Thomas Campbell and Joseph Steele, were convicted on highly circumstantial evidence, notably the testimony of William Love who said he overheard them in a pub talking about setting a fire. The 1984 jury believed him; it is doubtful whether a jury today would. Love has since recanted his evidence, saying he lied under pressure from two police officers who offered him a deal in return for evidence. At the time of writing, little has been done by the authorities to try and redress the wrong.

And so the longest-running murder trial in Scottish legal history came to an end. The court case and the investigation which preceded it had cost, according to one estimate, almost three million pounds but finally the man accused of the Arthur Thompson murder had been totally cleared and was now a free man. And he is still living and working in Glasgow today, despite rumours that there was a £30,000 contract on his life. ('The dogs on the street are barking that friends of Arthur Jnr have put up £30,000 to have him killed,' an anonymous 'top detective' told the *Daily Record*. The 'dogs on the street' did a lot of barking that year, it seems.)

Immediately after he emerged from the High Court of Glasgow to conduct a brief press conference, Paul Ferris was whisked away by representatives of the Scottish *Sun* to provide them with their exclusive story. On the way to a secret hideaway in the Highlands where the interview was conducted, the driver spotted two cars in pursuit. One, they reasoned, was filled with plainclothed police officers; the other with a group of unidentified men. Mindful of the contract said to be on their subject's head, they changed cars in Kinning Park, where the newspaper has its Glasgow headquarters, giving their pursuers the slip before speeding on north. Both parties have continued to insist that no money changed hands for the exclusive: Paul Ferris neither asked for nor was offered money. He spoke to the Scottish *Sun* because he trusted reporter Stephen Wilkie.

Meanwhile, it emerged that threats had been made against both the judge and the advocate-depute and both men had been placed under 24-hour police guard. The men who made those threats have never been caught.

Arthur Thompson Snr died on 13 March 1993. Much to the surprise of friends and enemies alike, he passed away in bed after a heart attack. Unknown to most people, he was already ill when he took the stand during the trial and knew he did not have much longer to live. He was buried beside his son and daughter in Riddrie cemetery, over 600 people attending the funeral. The night before the ceremony, army bomb-disposal experts exploded a suspicious device left at the grave site. It was a hoax. No one has yet stepped forward to claim his crown, although there are a number of young pretenders.

The police have not reopened their investigations into the murder of Arthur Thompson Jnr. The killers of Joseph Hanlon and Robert Glover are still at large. A report was supposedly lodged with the Crown Office but so far there have been no arrests.

Paul Ferris's name was not long out of the headlines. In the Old Bailey in August 1993, one of the men he named in his special defence of incrimination returned the favour by alleging that he had masterminded a Torquay bank raid. Michael Healy was standing trial along with five others for the failed raid committed in May 1991. He claimed that Ferris, along with the dead Hanlon and Glover, had planned the armed robbery. Another witness in the same trial, a former Glasgow criminal who now claimed to be a born-again Christian and named only as Mister A, even went as far as to claim that Mr Ferris had not only murdered Arthur Thompson Jnr, but also his friends Hanlon and Glover. There is no evidence to back this up, though.

Meanwhile, Robert Glover's widow has even turned to a medium for help. But apart from telling her to get on with her life, Bobby, speaking to her from the other side, could not name his killers. The dogs on the street might know who they are, but the spirit world, it seems, is as much in the dark as we are.

# Bibliography

Gaute, J.H.H. and Odell, Robin, *Murder Whatdunnit* (Pan), 1982

Glaister, Professor John, *Final Diagnosis* (Hutchinson), 1964

Hall, Angus (ed) *The Crimebusters* (Treasure Press), 1976

Lane, Brian, *The Encyclopedia of Forensic Science* (Headline), 1992

Murray Scott, Andrew and MacLeay, Iain, *Britain's Secret War* (Mainstream), 1990

Skelton, Douglas and Brownlie, Lisa, *Frightener: The Glasgow Ice-cream Wars* (Mainstream), 1992

Wilson, Richard, *Scotland's Unsolved Mysteries of the Twentieth Century* (Hale), 1989